# THE "SUCCESS" DICTIONARY

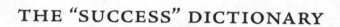

# THE "SUCCESS" DICTIONARY

Thoughts for change and imaginative thinking, from A to Z

Thomas S. Caldwell, C.M.

THIRD EDITION

Published by Caldwell Financial Ltd.
*The "Success" Dictionary: Thoughts for Change and Imaginative Thinking, from A to Z*, 3rd edition © 2018
Thomas S. Caldwell, c.m.

isbn 978-0-9683300-6-7 (pbk)
isbn 978-0-9683300-7-4 (electronic book)

Design: Peter Ross & Linda Gustafson / Counterpunch Inc.
Photography: Maria Gagliardi / marypics.com

Printed and bound in Canada by Friesens

Caldwell Financial Ltd.
150 King Street West, Suite 1702
po Box 47
Toronto, Ontario m5h 1j9
Canada
tcaldwell@caldwellsecurities.com

Dedicated to all the people I have known and worked with over the years. You are all in here in one way or another.

With thanks to my dear wife and tireless editor, Dorothy, for her support and patience.

I would also like to thank Elizabeth Naumovski, without whose help and hard work this book would not have been possible.

# About the Author

Thomas S. Caldwell's career in the investment industry began in 1965 after he graduated from McGill University with an honors degree in economics. He worked in research and sales in Montreal, New York and Toronto prior to founding Caldwell Securities Ltd. in 1980. As Chairman and Chief Executive Officer of Caldwell Financial Ltd., Mr. Caldwell now oversees brokerage and investment management activities in Canada and throughout the world. He is a past governor of the Toronto Stock Exchange and is internationally recognized as one of the leading authorities on securities exchange markets.

Mr. Caldwell is also CEO and a director of Urbana Corporation, a publicly traded investment company, and Chairman of the Canadian Securities Exchange ("the Exchange for Entrepreneurs").

In 2014, he was inducted into the IIAC Investment Industry Hall of Fame.

In 2012, Mr. Caldwell received the Queen Elizabeth II Diamond Jubilee Medal for his efforts on behalf of the disadvantaged. In 2003, he was appointed a Member of the Order of Canada for his work in assisting those in need, as well as for his contributions to institutions working to better the lives of others. In 2002, he was awarded the Queen Elizabeth II Golden Jubilee Medal for his activities on behalf of Canadian veterans. He is the Honorary Colonel of the Lincoln and Welland Regiment.

Says Caldwell: "Managing investments provides unique insights into the traits, habits and behaviors that lead to success across the spectrum of good and bad times."

# Introduction

First, let me state that this book comes from experiencing both success and adversity. No one is successful across all aspects of their lives. We all experience setbacks and heartbreaks. It is noteworthy that we learn more in adversity than in success. Difficulties and trials are opportunities for personal inventory, change and imaginative thinking.

In the following pages, you will see the key factors behind success and failure. The definitions or traits noted herein will help to polish and hone skills you already possess and combine them with the organization, discipline and character needed to succeed in life, no matter where you are now.

It is interesting to note that we are often our own greatest obstacles to success. This book attempts to deal with self-sabotage. The key factors for success are listed in dictionary form in order to be easily accessible. This book is meant to be used during your working day. Blank pages are included at the back for additional definitions that you find particularly helpful. Please feel free to forward them to me, for possible inclusion in future editions.

150 King Street West, Suite 1710
PO Box 47
Toronto, Ontario M5H 1J9
Canada
or tcaldwell@caldwellsecurities.com

# THE "SUCCESS" DICTIONARY

# A

**Abnormal**  Do not associate with people who consider abnormal normal.

**Abuse**  Do not tolerate it and do not inflict it.

**Acceptance**  Accept what you cannot change, but do not accept negatives as your lot in life. You were created to do things, not to be beaten down and immobilized.

**Accomplishments**  They are great and they build self-esteem and confidence. Do not, however, beat yourself up over things you did not do well. Accomplishments encourage the drive and determination to do better in the future. Each of us has unfinished business or unachieved goals in our past. They can be excellent fuel for future accomplishments.

**Accountable**  Be accountable in all matters. Do not shirk responsibility when things don't work out. To be a leader is to be accountable. Who are you accountable to?

**Achieve**  You can achieve anything you want, as long as you are prepared to go the distance and pay the price.

**Acting as If**  The "acting as if" behavior can be a powerful tool. "Acting as if" we will succeed is a way to practice being positive. It's a tool we can use to get ourselves unstuck.

"Acting as if" can be helpful when emotions begin to control us.

**Action**  You often hear the best ideas from people who never succeeded. The primary reason is that they never let their ideas stand the test of reality, usually because of fear. Ideas do not have to be great or inspired to bring success; they just have to be intelligently acted upon. Nothing happens until you get into action. Find reasons to act rather than to do nothing.

It is easier to act your way into better thinking than to think your way into better acting. If you are doing the "do" things, sooner or later your thinking will change and you will succeed.

**Action Freeze**   Usually fear of change or the need to be right underpins this success killer.

**Activist**   To succeed at anything you must be an activist. Get involved.

**Adamant**   Being adamant effectively shuts off constructive inputs and discussion. It alienates others and is a formula for isolation.

**Addictions**   They are easy to fall into and tough to get out of. Avoid playing with anything that has the potential to become obsessive and destructive.

**Adding**   What are you adding to the lives of others, to your company, to your country and to the world?

**Adversity**   Adversity seems to be a key ingredient for human progress. Only in troubles and conflict are we forced to really look at ourselves and our circumstances. Any serious investor will tell you that the bargains exist in adversity. That is also where the opportunities in life exist.

People often experience their greatest adversity just before their greatest success. Don't give up. Adversity is a wonderful teacher – if we pay attention.

**Advice**   Share what has or has not worked for you. Be wary of giving advice in matters you have not experienced. Listen to the advice of others and weigh it on the same basis.

Advice is not a commodity. It is not all of the same value.

**Afraid**  We should be afraid of not getting into action, of not acting on our good ideas.

**Age**  "I must say that I am too old to change."
– Ebenezer Scrooge
   Don't believe it. It wasn't true for him and it is not true for you. If you do not know who Scrooge is, start reading good books.

No matter what your age or condition, always try to be accomplishing something. This does not include improving your golf or tennis game.

"How old would you be if you didn't know how old you are?" – Satchel Paige

**Agenda**  It is virtually impossible to work with people who have an agenda apart from the agreed-upon common goal.

**Agendas**  Never have two agendas for any meeting. Chase one rabbit and catch it. Chase two and nothing will be achieved.

**Aggressiveness**  Aggressive behavior often suggests desperation. Be aggressive but don't show it.

**Agreements**  They must always be strictly adhered to, with no unilateral changes or rationalizations.

**Alcohol**  The best way to make a difficult situation appear insurmountable is to pour alcohol on top of it. Drinking plays a key role in many suicides. The lack of perspective resulting from alcohol use can have less dramatic, but still negative, outcomes. Also, the time, opportunities, self-esteem and relationships put at risk strongly suggest the need to watch for this subtle and patient destroyer.

**Alive**  Find a vocation that makes you "come alive." You will then be good at it.

**Alternatives**  Listen or suffer. Pay attention to good advice or suffer the consequences of your actions. The former is easy. The latter generally involves pain.

**Ambition** Ambition is a good thing, but try not to let it stand in the way of accomplishment. Ambition relates to self. Accomplishment usually relates to others and a common goal.

**Amends** Don't mess up making amends by making excuses.

**Amnesia** Selective amnesia is a common phenomenon. Do not expect total recall from people with agendas or attitudes.

**Anger** Anger alienates, isolates and eventually consumes. Do not use anger as fuel for thinking or behavior. Anger is often fear based.

Try to replace anger with introspection. What was your part?

**Answer** Be the answer to someone else's prayer.

**Anticipate** Try to anticipate the anticipators, to be "ahead of the curve." Attempt to understand where events or a course of action are leading. This can avoid pain and lead to gain.

**Anxiety** Everyone suffers from anxiety to some degree, whether or not it is based on reality. We usually have very little control over the stimuli affecting our emotions, but the net result of unchecked anxiety is highly destructive. It can literally immobilize a person and lead to the very outcome that is most feared.

The best counter to anxiety is to attempt to take your eyes off yourself or your circumstances and try to find a way to be of service or help to someone else. The key is to trust that your needs will be met as you help others to meet theirs.

**Apologies** If you make a mistake, apologize and make amends quickly. Clean things up and move on.

**Appetites** Trim your appetites.

**Appreciation** Show it. If you do not appreciate a relationship or anything else, you will lose it.

**Approachable** Always be approachable. That's how you get good ideas.

**Arrogance** It is the one trait guaranteed to alienate. For leaders, the opposite of arrogance is not humility but empathy, that is, appreciating how one's attitudes and behaviors affect others. Arrogant people are unteachable.

**Ask** "Why?" often. "How?" is also good. There are no foolish questions, unless they are simply attempts to be noticed. The legitimate quest for knowledge and information is normally respected. Try to discern the real underlying factors in the events affecting you.

**Assets** Your two key assets are expertise and time. If you waste time, your expertise will not matter.

**Assign** Assigning tasks is the only way to get extra leverage from your time and ideas. Remember, however, that as responsibilities are assigned down the line, they become less important to each subsequent individual.

Follow-up is key to ensuring that things get done.

**Assume**  Assume positive behavior and responses from others. Even when you do not receive them, act as if you have. It is amazing how a negative situation can be turned around with positive responses and acts of kindness, consideration and humor.

**Attack**  Always be on the attack – especially when in doubt. Get going. Nothing happens until you get into action.

**Attitude**  What actually happens to or around you is not as important as your attitude when it does. There is some good in everything and everyone in this life, yet nothing and no one is perfect. We have, as a consequence, a choice in the way we look at things. Your attitude is the single most important factor in determining the outcome of any situation or endeavor. It is more important than skills, training, background or anything else.

**Attraction**  Attraction rather than self-promotion is the best way to build and establish relationships. Be enthusiastic and upbeat about your work, your company, your associates and your friends. You will be amazed how people are then drawn to you.

**Availability**  Being involved in life will put you in contact with others. People are interested in what others do, and like to deal with or be with those they know and respect. The more activities you are involved in, the greater will be your availability to others.

Availability is almost as important as ability.

# B

**Bad Behavior**  Never blame people, places or things for your own bad behavior. Smarten up, clean it up and move on – a bit wiser.

**Bad Habits**  Try to spot them and deal with them.

**Bad Ideas**  They can only be fought with better ideas.

**Basics**  Master the basics of any endeavor.

**Battles**  The big ones are within ourselves. As we deal with those, the external ones become easier.

**Be**  To be a great person is not the same as having accomplished great things. Society often confuses the two. Often the latter can distract from the former.

**Beauty** Anyone can have inner beauty.

**Behavior** Always conduct yourself so that it would not matter if your actions were shown on television. Strive to be consistent with what you say. What you do says more about you than what you say.

Never let your behavior transcend the event. This can happen when something goes wrong and one responds with rage. Instantly, the individual and their behavior become the focus, not the lesson to be learned or even the corrective action to be taken. Bad behavior is always "justifiable."

**Believe** Believe in yourself, your skills and your own integrity. Without the assurance that comes from this, your results will be mediocre at best. Believe that God wants you to do your best to be of service to others. This conviction will see you through many sparse and dark periods.

**Best**  Do your best each day. Don't be half-baked in your approach to life, business or anything else. The results from doing your best (or even trying to) are totally predictable.

**Betrayal**  You will not get through life without experiencing betrayal. It is a hard if not devastating thing, particularly if the person who betrayed you was close or someone you have helped. Just try to remember that everyone is fallible, and we all have let people down. As for that small percentage who are pathological, it is better to have them out of your life, whatever the cost.

**Better**  Never lose the drive to be better, or to make things better.

**Bible**  The Bible specifically addresses every area of human need. Someone once described it as "the Manufacturer's Handbook" and, as such, it has all the instructions we require. Even for agnostics, it can be considered the accumulation of wisdom over the ages. This valuable resource should not be ignored, in either good or bad times. The Bible is also filled with flawed characters, just like us, who often did great things.

**Bigger** Think bigger than your surroundings or current activities. View your life in a far larger context than simply the things you are doing or experiencing. See yourself in terms of history and great accomplishments, and, if possible, in reference to what God might have in mind for you. This is what determines greatness. Set yourself on a path to accomplish extraordinary things.

**Bitterness** Fight it like the plague. It can and will devour everything else in life. The only known antidote is forgiveness. Avoid bitterness at all costs.

**Blame** Blaming others is almost a certain guarantee that you will not learn or progress from setbacks. Ask yourself what your part in the problem was and how you can change or benefit from it. Get out of the blame game.

**Blasé** Blasé attitudes and behavior have a cost.

**Blessed**  We are blessed so that we can bless others.

**Bonding**  We usually bond with people when we have common experiences or do things together. Get together in some format with friends, customers and prospects to develop relationships.

**Books**  Nonfiction is vastly more beneficial than fiction. You want to know what real people did in real circumstances, and how it worked out. This can provide both encouragement and a basis for identification. History is a great teacher. It is a pity that we so thoroughly ignore it or mutilate it.

**Bore**  Simply put, don't bore people. Provide ideas, humor, encouragement and so on, but don't pound people into the ground with excess verbiage or continual repetition.

**Born**  Just because you may have been born on third base doesn't mean you hit a triple.

**Bounce Back**  "Success is how high you bounce when you hit bottom." – General George S. Patton

**Box** Always try to think "outside the box." Look at things in a nonconventional way. That is how inspiration and innovation occur.

**Brain** Sometimes half of our brain manufactures rubbish, and the other half buys it. Question your thinking occasionally.

**Breaks** We seem to get the breaks only when we need them.

**Break-Up** It seems that only after the break-up of a business or a personal relationship do we see those things we could have, or should have, done. Try to consider positive actions before a break-up. Look ahead and see the other person's point of view.

**Brevity** Speeches and meetings should be kept short, with easy-to-remember key points. Everyone knows and is inspired by Lincoln's Gettysburg Address, and no one recalls the several-hour speech that preceded it, nor the individual who made it.

**Build** You want to be building, not just living. Be a builder of people and organizations. You cannot build if you get used to tearing things or people down.

**Burdens** Travel light.

**Business Success** There are three key ingredients: value, service and communication. "I am a business success by virtue of the facts that I love what I do and I love the people I do it with." – T. S. Caldwell

**Busy** Busy is not the same as productive. Check yourself as to the potential real results of your "busy" activities.

# C

**Call Back** Do not assume the reason for a person's call. Call them back. You will often be surprised. Returning calls is a form of advertising. It establishes your courtesy, efficiency and attitude. No one is so important they cannot return all calls by the end of the business day.

**Can Be** Never invest on the basis of "what is" or how a thing or an investment looks now. Think in terms of what can be.

**Can Do** You do not know what you can do until you have to do it.

**Can't** "Can't" is a word that should be rarely used. Be honest with yourself and use the word you really mean: "won't." The more you won't do, the more you can't do.

**Capability** The less you do, the less you are capable of doing. If you are not exercising your "mental muscles" on small tasks, you will not be up to the bigger ones. This is a variant on the old maxim "If you want something done, give it to a busy person."

**Care** Care for others whenever and however you can. You may be surprised by how it enriches your own life. It is one of life's truths that we are blessed when we bless others.

**Career** Remember that character is more important than career. If you build your character, your career will follow.

**Careerist** Someone who sees a job as simply a means to getting a better one. Consistently doing the best you can is probably one of the better methods of advancement. This means putting a high value on one's job, customers and fellow workers. Going for short-term glory or opportunity in order to move on breeds resentment from all quarters. Careerists are seen as time wasters as soon as their real motivation is understood.

**Career Killers**  Attitude, anger, arrogance and adamance.

**Cash**  It is occasionally a valid investment alternative.

**Casual**  Do not be casual in your dress, your attitudes or your work. People should expect your best at all times and not be disappointed.

**Cemented**  Do not become cemented into your views and attitudes.

**Center**  Get yourself out of the center of the universe and put God, as you understand Him, there and then try to live your life with reference to Him.

**Challenge**  Occasionally, it is important to challenge your own thinking.

**Change** Money is made from change. Correctly anticipating changing events, circumstances or perceptions can be very profitable. Also, try to be an agent for positive change.

**Chaos** Do not get emotionally drawn in but look for the possibilities and opportunities existing within chaos. At a minimum, try to learn from it. Respond, don't react.

**Character** Character is defined and built in adversity, not success. "The first thing is character, before money or property or anything else." – J. P. Morgan

Character is what defines us as individuals. It is our fundamental operating system. Aspiring to be a person of integrity forms our character and defines our reputation. Character determines what we do without thinking.

**Charity** Charity begins at home, then works its way out from there. Sometimes it is harder to be charitable with family, and that is why it should be the starting point.

Giving consideration, time and funds to help others is always a good investment. It will also define you (primarily to yourself) as a winner.

Charity is a mindset toward others. Giving for recognition is simply an ego-feeding exercise. If you are not kind and caring within your family, then the good things you do outside it are just ego or show, or both.

**Cheating** To think cheating is clever is simply delusional. The results are totally predictable.

**Children** When they are young, give them unconditional love. When they are older, add forgiveness, because they won't remember your unconditional love for them.

**Choice** Each day, you choose what you are going to do or what you will attempt. If you do not make this conscious choice, it will be made for you by circumstances, events or others. You can choose what you are going to think or worry about. You can also choose to be positive.

**Choices** You always have them. Do not make yours based on habits or emotions – you always have choices when dealing with unpleasant people or difficult situations. Sadly, many people seem to be hardwired for an anger response.

**Circumstances** Your current situation or circumstance is not necessarily an indicator of your future possibilities. Your situation is a reflection of what has gone on before, but attitudes, focus, change, skills, faith, effort and determination are what will decide the future.

**Clarity** Usually we require a moment of clarity or an "epiphany" in order to change. Try to spot and grow from those moments. Strive for clarity of thought and word.

**Clean** Clean yourself up. Recognize and come to grips with character defects such as low self-esteem, fear and the craving for acceptance from others, which continually sabotage ability. Externals such as appearance are also important.

**Close the Loop**  Because all of our actions are inter-related, items left undone or not communicated can cost both time and money.

When working on any project, or giving instructions, one should make sure everyone involved is clearly informed. Organizations or teams can only excel if members "close the loop."

**Clutter**  Continually work at "decluttering" your life – of unnecessary stuff, difficult relationships and bad ideas.

**Coercion**  Coercion is the crudest and lowest form of influence. Avoid it as much as possible.

**Cold**  Cold or aloof people generally do not add much to life. Try to be involved and to contribute.

**Comfort Zone**  Success and growth come from stretching yourself and reaching into new and sometimes uncomfortable situations. Get out of your comfort zone and it will expand. No one ever became successful staying in their comfort zone.

**Comments**  First ask yourself, Does anything need to be said? Is now the time to say it? Am I the one to say it?

**Commitment**  Commitment to your own success is necessary. You must root out those things (external and internal) that stand in the way of true progress. Commitment will keep you going when others fall by the wayside.

**Commitments**  They must always be kept. Your word and your reputation must be as solid as a rock.

**Committee**  "A committee is a group that keeps minutes and loses hours." – Milton Berle

**Common Sense**  It can save a great deal of wasted time and effort. Why are you doing a thing? What is the goal? Is it reasonable? Can it be explained easily? Be careful when things are too complicated.

**Communicate**  Express your ideas and/or information in a manner others can understand and relate to. Professionals and salespeople often use the jargon of their particular trades, which many people simply do not understand.

Communicating clearly and effectively is also critical to the internal functioning of any organization. All companies are in the communications business, both internally and externally.

**Compare** "If you compare yourself with others, you may become vain or bitter." – *Desiderata*

**Compassion** Compassion is what defines us as human.

**Competitive** In your corporate life be competitive externally, not internally.

**Complaints** Always be positive when making them. Do not challenge or threaten. Simply try to help people see the situation, and get yourself and your emotions out of it. Humor sometimes helps.

When receiving complaints, forget your ego, then see and address the person's concerns and needs to the best of your ability.

**Complexity**  Complexity is the enemy of execution.

**Compromise**  If you do not stick to what you know is right, you kill your self-esteem, the respect of others and the momentum required for victory. Do not be afraid to change your stance if you are not right.

**Computers**  They know everything but understand nothing.

**Concentrate**  Focus on your goal, and the steps to achieving it, on an hourly, daily, weekly or yearly basis. Be ruthless with distractions, no matter how alluring. Concentrate on the means of success, not the symptoms of failure.

**Confidence**  Confidence comes from believing that you are doing the right thing. Confidence is central to leadership. If you do not have confidence in yourself, no one else will.

**Conflicts** Try to stand back and weigh what is going on before getting involved. If you do enter in, keep personalities and blame out of it. If you can't help out – stay out.

**Confront** Confront your lesser fears (e.g., rejection), or the bigger ones (e.g., failure) will overtake you.

**Confusion** We are often the most confused at turning points. Try to see what is really important within the information you have. Where will the different decisions lead? Common sense and what is right are great guides.

**Connect** Connect with others, even if it is only to say "Good morning." Use the other person's name if possible. You can improve someone else's day simply by greeting him or her. Make a point of doing it. This, in turn, will establish you as a caring and interested person. Connecting with and relating to people is the initial building block for all relationships. You cannot truly connect if you are trying to impress.

**Consequences**  Our decisions, actions (or lack thereof) and attitudes always have consequences. Think ahead to them.

**Consideration**  The Golden Rule: Treat others as you wish to be treated. The backlash from inconsiderate behavior is predictable and can have a negative impact on your reputation, relationships and business. Seeing people as important is the key to being of service to others. This is what business, and life, are all about.

**Consistency**  Strive to be consistent in your actions and statements. A reputation for dependability and trustworthiness comes from consistent behavior. It is a terrific asset.

**Conspicuous Consumption**  Although one should appear successful, try to avoid going "over the top." That only makes a person look ridiculous.

**Contingencies**  Expect them and plan for them.

**Contrarian**  Try to look at things differently from the masses. You may see some possibilities.

**Control**  There is not a lot in life one can control, and particularly not people. Trying to control the lives of others will lead directly to rebellion and alienation. This especially includes our children. Move on to things you can do something about.

**Convergence**  You become what you do.

**Convince**  Only the pain of living can convince a person to change. As a friend, one can share "how to change," but we cannot provide the motivation to change.

**Cool**  Do not lose yours – in any circumstance.

**Cooperate**  Virtually all success is the result of a group effort. That means cooperation. "Cooperate" is one of the words children's TV programs used to stress. Its meaning should probably be retaught to adults.

**Corporate Diversity**  Hire the best people and diversity will take care of itself.

**Correct**  Correct people with kindness, and always leave them room to still feel good about themselves, you and the organization.

**Correspondence**  Keep it simple and short.

**Count On**  Be the sort of person that people can count on, and associate with people who can be counted on.

**Courage**  Courage and honesty go together. This includes the willingness to look honestly at ourselves. Have the courage to change, to admit mistakes and to praise others. We are not talking about the courage to charge up a hill, but to confront our own fears and insecurities. This is tougher stuff than mere physical daring.

**Courtesy**  Be courteous and considerate to everyone. It costs nothing yet pays significant dividends.

Think about the effect of your action and inactions on others. Courtesy is professionalism in action.

**Crazy**  The test for good business associates is that you are not all crazy on the same day.

**Creativity**  Creativity should become a core competency. All businesses are built on the basis of intellectual superiority, combined with the ability to execute.

**Credit**  It is hard to give credit to someone who has already grabbed it all.

**Criticism**  People generally find that it is much easier to be against things than to be part of a group or process to make things better. Look for what is right or good and try to build on the existing positives: it is an exercise in maturity. Criticize actions or events, not the people themselves. But first determine if the issue is important enough. Leave people room to save face.

**Critics**  They don't count. "The credit belongs to the man who is actually in the arena ... and spends himself in a worthy cause; who at best, if he wins, knows the thrills of high achievement, and, if he fails, at least fails daring greatly, so that his place shall never be with those cold and timid souls who know neither victory or defeat."
– Theodore Roosevelt

"Critics are men who watch a battle from a high place then come down and shoot the survivors."
– Ernest Hemingway

**Cruel**  Occasionally, you have to be cruel to be kind. That is the only excuse for cruelty.

**Cumulative**  Doing the "right thing" consistently will eventually bring positive results.

**Curiosity**  Keep a sense of curiosity as to people, how things work and why things are as they are. Innovators all have inquiring minds.

# D

**Debating** Debating is about winning and is inherently dishonest, as disagreeable information is often debased. Debating can be counterproductive in the real world, as it shuts off inputs and alienates.

Not every discussion has to be a debate. Elicit ideas and seek understanding. Get ego and personality to the sidelines. Treat those who oppose you with respect and, if possible, good humor.

**Debt** Try to restrict your borrowings to the purchase of long-term assets, which have the realistic potential of appreciating in value. Borrowing for current expenses or to buy depreciating assets will eventually come back to haunt you.

**Decisions** If you have to make an important decision, try these three steps:

First, pray. You want to be in line with God's will and seek His direction. If you do not have a faith, pray anyway. At a minimum, you will hear yourself more honestly articulate the alternatives.

Second, talk to someone else. Most of us are rationalizers and should seek an outside opinion in order to ensure our wants or emotions are not coloring our view of things.

Third, wait until your choice "feels comfortable." Sometimes, deep down, as a result of a number of small factors, we know the answer. This is the root of common sense. These steps help to quell emotions before making decisions.

Never make an important decision in front of anyone else. Getting back to someone may cause you to miss the occasional deal, but using these steps will dramatically improve the quality and results of your decision making. A nondecision is still a decision. Good decisions justify themselves.

Decisions and commitments are the same thing.

**Defeat** Defeat exists only when it is accepted. The seeds of victory are within every setback. Get the positives out of every negative, i.e., learn.

**Defeatist** Defeatist thinking is learned. It can be unlearned. Try to be positive and enthusiastic about yourself, your prospects and what you can do to help others.

**Defensive** Do not be defensive in your reactions. Most often, comments from others are not meant to hurt. Defensive people cut themselves off, as others won't risk their response. Defensive people cannot be taught.

**Degrees** Don't take them too seriously, particularly if you have one or more. Degrees can be helpful in government or teaching, but in the real world, determination, common sense and a clear sense of right and wrong are the requirements for success.

**Delegate** It is the only way to leverage one's intellect, skills and overall abilities.

**Demonization** In order to treat people badly, it is first necessary to demonize or diminish them. Individuals and countries all play at this. It is justification through vilification. It will happen to you over your lifetime. You are not alone.

**Denial** Whatever is denied cannot be fixed. Before a problem can be addressed and corrected, it must be seen to exist. Denial is a great barrier to all progress, personal or corporate.

**Dependability** Business is based on trust. "On time, on budget and as promised" is the norm for successful careers and enterprises. When given an instruction, carry it out fully and report back, especially if there are problems. Dependability and greater responsibility go together.

**Deprecate** Never deprecate or belittle an individual just because they will not do or be what you want them to do or be. That is not your role in life. Do not do it under any circumstances. Name calling is part of this.

**Depressed or Depression** The counters are gratitude and helping others.

**Desire** Before anything is attempted or accomplished, there must be desire. If strong enough, desire will supplant all distractions and substitutes, and compel us to drive to its end. What do you really desire and why?

**Despair** Many great leaders suffer from periods of despondency and despair. Winston Churchill called it "the black dog of despair." When going through this sort of thing, remember that you have something in common with Churchill and other greats.

**Desperate** A desperate person does desperate things and makes bad decisions. Don't be one and don't deal with one.

**Destructive Thinking** This is exemplified when gratitude is replaced with entitlement, enthusiasm is replaced with anger, and the team or group effort is replaced with self. The results are not hard to predict.

**Determination**  Determination is often the decider of success or failure. If you are on the right path, stay determined.

**Differences**  We are not all the same, despite modern pressures to think so. Differing values, attitudes, interests and abilities are what define us as human. What should be a constant is respect for all.

**Difficulties**  They plague everyone from time to time. Deal with them the best way you can. Breaking them down into bite-size pieces can sometimes help. Trying to avoid difficulties very often leads to bigger problems.

**Diminish**  Never diminish others. It only diminishes you. Those who put down others usually need to do so in order to feel better about themselves.

**Directors**  High-profile corporate directors are normally overconcerned with their own reputations. They are the first ones to turn or bolt in tough times.

**Disadvantage** Always look for a way to use your perceived disadvantage as an advantage. A disadvantage can force you to find a better way of doing things.

**Disagreements** They can be positive if the goal is to grow or learn. To get there, anger and egos must be shelved.

**Disappointment** Not everything in life will turn out as you wish. This is just part of life. Very often, when we look back, we are relieved we didn't get what we wanted. Move on in the belief that things will work out as they should, and don't get bogged down with individual disappointments.

**Disappointments** We all have them, and we all create them.

**Disasters** They usually result from some combination of ego, momentum, poor communication and lack of information.

**Discernment**  Try to discern the difference between what a person is saying and what that person is really telling you. There is often a world of difference. Understanding the difference is crucial to both interpersonal and business success.

**Discipline**  Discipline is internal. It is how we rule ourselves, our emotions, our fatigue, our hunger, etc. Doing what should be done is the result of internal discipline, not of the discipline itself. Self-discipline and self-esteem are connected.

**Discouragement**  "This too shall pass."
  A few steps that can help:
  + View your present situation as temporary.
  + Do your best, one day at a time.
  + Ask for help – pray if possible.
  + Have faith. Believe that things will
    get better.
  + Ask yourself: What is the next positive thing
    I can do?

**Discussions** Discussions should be an honest exchange of ideas. That implies getting all you can from the other participant(s).

**Dishonest** Truly dishonest people actually believe their own lies. They are pathological. Then there are those who know they are lying but are driven by fear or anger. Don't be, or associate with, either.

Dishonest people think everyone else is like them. An ongoing lack of honesty eventually deadens one's conscience.

**Disillusionment** We are not in charge of, or responsible for, the behavior of others. All of us have let people down. We are all fallible. Get over it.

**Dislike** Do the things you dislike or don't want to do. This is how a person grows in skill, strength and character.

**Disloyalty** Assuming it assures it. Never rationalize being disloyal.

**Dismiss**  Do not dismiss or laugh at your failings. Recognize them with self-honesty and deal with them, no matter how trivial they may seem. If you don't, they will eventually deal with you.

**Dismissive**  Do not handle the concerns or even complaints of others in a dismissive, casual or demeaning manner. It will exacerbate the issue and establish you as both uncaring and arrogant.

**Disorganized**  Disorganized people are always overworked, not the other way around.

**Distractions**  Be ruthless with distractions. Do not use them to procrastinate.

**Distrust**  Distrustful people usually judge others by their own standards. They are telling you about their thought processes and intent.

**Division**  There are people who continually sow division and discord. It is almost as if they need to create a soap opera, or they seek to use office politics to get to the top. Don't keep them in your life.

**Do** Do the "do" things and you will be amazed at how things work out.

**Doing** Success comes more from doing than knowing. Even a mediocre idea can work, if acted upon intelligently.

If you keep doing what you have been doing, you are going to keep getting what you have been getting.

**"Don't Care"** People who say they "don't care" often care a great deal.

**Doubt** Self-doubt can undermine your intentions and efforts. Try to replace doubt with confidence, optimism and faith as quickly as you can. Make changes if you have to, but keep moving forward expecting success.

**Drama** There is already enough drama in life; don't create more.

**Dream** If you are going to dream, dream big – then get on with it.

**Dress** Dress conservatively. You can be assured that others will be looking at your suit, hair, shoes, etc., grasping for some tip-off as to your personality, maturity and success.

Do not overdo the image thing, but don't sabotage yourself before letting your ideas and ability establish your caliber. Dress often indicates what you think of yourself and others.

**Drugs** If you use chemicals to live in the real world, you have a problem. It doesn't matter if you pop them, sip them, shoot them or smoke them. (*See also* **Alcohol**.)

# E

**"Es"**  The four Es of success are Ethics, Empathy, Energy and Extra.

**Early**  Be early for meetings, but don't worry about being first to do everything. Remember, it is the second mouse that gets the cheese.

**Easier**  Try to find an easier way to do things. That does not mean being shoddy or cutting corners. It means striving for efficiency.

**Eat**  Learn to eat properly. This includes how you hold your knife and fork, keeping your mouth shut while chewing and not making eating noises. Do not stuff your mouth with food and do not lick your fingers. If you do not address these issues, you will never really know why you didn't get that second date or the promotion you desired. No one will tell you these things because they are too embarrassing.

**Effort** Always give things 100 percent of your time, effort and energy, or don't bother. A 90 percent effort leaves 10 percent to cause chaos and resentment in an interdependent environment or team effort such as business.

Do not rationalize poor effort on the basis of a change in priorities. Occasionally, great effort is required for even modest results. Do not be discouraged. Keep at it and you will break out into easier going.

**Emotionally Needy** People with this trait need continual affirmation, praise and recognition – almost to the point of needing to feel worshipped. They can drain relationships, teams and efforts. It is almost impossible to fill their void, but sometimes its destructiveness can be moderated with a bit of praise and recognition. Most people are emotionally needy at some level; the degree to which they are is key.

**Emotions** Emotions cost money. Leaders must learn to quell their emotions. This is particularly important when making decisions.

**Empathy** An intuitive understanding of and caring about the needs and feelings of others. Empathy inspires loyalty.

**Enablers** Those who protect others from the consequences of their actions or insulate them from reality usually end up making matters much worse. Enablers can kill others with their supposed kindness.

**Encourage** This is the best way to get the full potential from your fellow workers, team members or friends. Be part of the success of others. There is no more important role in life than that of an "encourager."

**End** What we often see as the end is often the beginning of something better.

"Everything will be all right in the end and if it's not all right, then it's not yet the end." – Sonny Kapoor character, *The Best Exotic Marigold Hotel*

**Endeavor**  It is part of human nature. Deep down, we must always be doing something, striving and moving forward. Always have a vision or goal.

**Enemies**  Often they are people you have helped, who cannot forgive you for doing so. Yet, the enemy within is always the most dangerous and destructive.

"We have met the enemy … and he is us." – *Pogo* cartoon

**Energy**  If you lack the strength to keep going, get into action – do something even slightly productive and you will be surprised how your energy comes back. To succeed at anything, one must develop and maintain a high energy level.

**Enjoy**  Make it a point to enjoy life. Remember, many people on the *Titanic* turned down dessert.

**Enthusiasm**  In the final analysis, enthusiasm is infectious. If you do not have enthusiasm between an opportunity and success, you have a brick wall.

**Entitlement**  This is probably the dominant attitude in Western society, and it is indicative of a lack of gratitude. Never confuse generosity with entitlement.

Entitlement comes from placing ourselves at the center of the universe and subconsciously demanding what we feel we are due. Get over it; we are owed nothing and we are responsible for our own actions, whatever the outcome.

A sense of entitlement always leads to rebellion. You are entitled to nothing. Earn what you expect.

**Entrepreneurs**  They turn possibilities into realities, and concepts into jobs and economic progress. Entrepreneurs are the highest rung in the free enterprise system.

**Epic** Everyone wants to be part of an epic event. We can be, a little bit at a time, by helping others and changing lives.

**Escapism** Escapism comes in many guises. It can take the form of substitute accomplishments, good works, family and social commitments or a focus on micro-issues. Try to recognize it and get back on track.

**Ethics** It is easy to be ethical in calm, prosperous times. The acid test comes when under the stress of adversity. That defines a person.

Most people know right from wrong. Be clear on what you stand for, then be consistent in your action.

**Evaluate** Examine your efforts and results on a daily basis. What did you do and what did you achieve? This daily exercise will help to cut down on substitutes and procrastination.

Evaluate but do not judge. The latter implies a sense of superiority on your part.

**Events** They can be spurs to action or guides for direction. See both good and bad situations in this manner.

**Everything** People who have been given everything often try to believe they have been given nothing. It is a self-esteem issue, so do not expect gratitude from them.

**Exaggerate** Neither exaggerate nor minimize. Aim for expressing reality, and self-honesty.

**Example** The best way to influence others is through being a positive example.

**Excellence** Excellence is an ongoing, daily process. It pertains to both small and large endeavors, and it is a torment of sorts.

**Excess** You can neither spend yourself solvent nor drink yourself sober.

**Excuses**  Recognize the difference between excuses and reasons. Make excuses for others, not yourself.

Making excuses is easy. Taking action is harder. If you find yourself continually making excuses for poor or nonperformance, you are either dishonest or disorganized, or both. And that is certainly how you will be perceived.

**Execution**  A vision and a plan are two legs of a three-legged stool. Without execution, the other two are irrelevant. Execution is, in great measure, a sales exercise, that is, communicating an idea, concept or product advantage in order to influence others' thinking and actions.

**Exercise**  Regular physical exercise is essential to long-term success. Get into a routine and you will find it helps with tension, fear, anxiety and low self-esteem. Your brain will also work better.

You cannot "out-exercise" what you eat.

**Expand**  Expand your world. Be part of a world larger than your business interests or job. Be of service in the wider spectrum of life. Numerous friends and contacts will result.

**Expectations**  It is a good thing to have high expectations of yourself – and to exceed them. But if you have high expectations of others, you will be disappointed. Having expectations of others' and their behavior may actually be a premeditated resentment.

**Expediency**  Expediency should never replace ethics and doing a thing well.

**Experience**  Experience is invaluable if we benefit from it and use it to help ourselves or others. Very little in our lives is ever wasted, and even the difficult things we suffer through can be used in some positive way.

**Experts**  Beware of them and do not be intimidated by them. Specific knowledge is often necessary, but it should not be confused with common sense or wisdom. Experts sometimes get confused in this matter, as do those who are mesmerized by them.

**Extend**  Extend yourself, your reach and your abilities. Try to do that extra push-up, jog that extra hundred yards or do slightly more than you have been able to accomplish in the past. You don't need to climb mountains every weekend, but push slightly beyond your norm. By doing so, your abilities, confidence and sense of self-worth will grow.

**External**  Never blame your situation on external events or other people. If you do, you will not learn.

**Extra**  Always try to go that extra mile. This behavior is what loyalty is built on. Giving the extra can overcome most competitive disadvantages. To some extent, this means putting your faith in people to respond. Occasionally you will be let down, but in the long run your effort will be rewarded.

**Extrapolate**  Do not extrapolate or extend the present into the future. You can change the future by your actions.

**Extremes**  Avoid extremes in thought, word and deed. They point to immaturity and an unwillingness to be open or to learn. They also scare people.

# F

**Faces**  Behind every face is a story. Older faces have longer stories. Try to see the stories.

**Failings**  People rarely see the failings of others in themselves. We all like to preserve our self-image.

**Failure**  To be a failure requires making many wrong decisions over a prolonged period, and then giving up. Failure is not a one-decision thing.

What most people call failures are really just set-backs. The seeds of victory are within every setback.

**Fair**  Be fair in all your dealings. This includes with suppliers. Pay a fair price and do not grind people down. Also pay on a timely basis. You want to be a good customer.

**Faith** Faith has been described as the "substance of things hoped for." Anyone who has played a sport or been in a game has experienced this, especially when the score is against you.

Faith is often suddenly knowing you can win. It is a confidence that speaks clearly, revitalizes and often leads to victory. Work on building faith in your God, yourself and what you are doing. It is a clear path to victory, and not much happens without it.

Faith is your best weapon against despair in adversity. It should be in place before the trouble begins, just as defenses should be built up before an attack. There is little time to do so during the event.

**Faked Out** Do not get faked out or faked in. Stay cool.

**Family** Family goals should be part of your career goals and vice versa. Our families can provide great joy as well as great pain, and most of us experience both over a lifetime.

We are, however, responsible to our families and for their welfare. Do not use them as excuses for half-hearted business efforts.

**Family Business**  All families are dysfunctional to some degree, and family members usually have some historic issues. Importing these issues into a business environment can be highly destructive. Be extremely cautious when bringing family into a business. To work effectively, a family business should treat every employee, whether family or not, as a member of the family.

**Fatigue**  Emotional or physical fatigue magnifies the tasks facing us and diminishes our ability and resolve to deal with them. Very often, however, it is a symptom rather than a cause. Procrastination evaporates energy. Action, however small, is often the antidote for fatigue.

Fatigue can also cause us to see others as irritations or interruptions. Watch for this; it is a symptom of burnout.

**Fault** Your life is no one else's fault. It is yours!

**Favoritism** This can be the undoing of any leader or organization. It does not preclude helping someone in need or rewarding a person who has done an outstanding job.

Employees have the right to expect the fairness of a meritocracy. Unwarranted favoring of family or friends can be a morale disaster.

**Fear** Fear can immobilize anyone. Separate real fear from irrational fear. Real fear is a warning bell; irrational fear usually needs to be fed by lack of confidence, or often something as simple as fatigue.

When confronted with real fear, shrink your time frame to one day or one hour, etc. Anyone can handle virtually anything in small amounts. It is only when we extrapolate into the future, or look back, that we have difficulty.

Many of us must wrestle with fear on a regular basis.

**Feel Good**  Try to do well, or the right thing, first, then see if you don't "feel good." Feeling good is a by-product.

**Feeling Badly**  Possibly you should. Check if there is something that needs to be corrected or dealt with. If you are feeling badly about yourself, do not let your first step be denial or defensiveness.

**F.I.D.O.**  "Forget it, drive on." Do not hang on to old hurts and grudges. Keep moving forward and try to leave those burdens behind you.

**Fighting**  "I will fight no more forever." – Chief Joseph of the Nez Perce
Not a bad sentiment.

**Figure It Out**  If something does not immediately work, figure it out. Develop an inquiring mind and calm your emotions in order to come at the problem again (and again).

**Filler**  What do you fill your time with? Is it productive?

**Financial Problems**  Financial problems rarely exist. Financial symptoms are the norm. What we see as a problem is, in reality, often a symptom of a real underlying problem. For individuals, the real or underlying problem can be alcohol, drugs, attitudes, focus, etc. In regard to companies, it can be product, services, courtesy, location, lack of customer appreciation, etc. Find and deal with the "real" problem, and financial symptoms will evaporate.

**Fire**  You cannot instill fire, passion or enthusiasm in others unless you have it yourself, and communicate it effectively in both words and actions.

**First Class**  Think and act first class in all things and at all times.

**First Impressions**  How many times can you make a first impression? A bad first impression is very difficult to overcome. It is far easier to arrive appropriately dressed and well spoken than to have to engage in damage control later.

**Fitness** We are mental, physical and spiritual beings who require exercise, rest and nutrition in each of these areas. Look at your attitudes, emotions and habits, as well as at the operating basis for your life. In order to achieve excellence throughout a career and lifetime, long-term fitness across this threefold spectrum is mandatory. Deal with those things that you know to be harmful.

**Flags** In the prospect's mind, poor grammar, coarse language, and sloppy dress or appearance all raise flags as to your caliber or level of professionalism.

**Flat Periods** For achievers, flat periods are very hard. We all go through these times in life and business. Just focus on your goals, inch toward them and do not get discouraged by seemingly slow or no progress. These periods are just a pause for us to sort things out. Make sure they stay just a pause.

**Focus** Focus externally. Try to be of service to others, and help them with their needs and concerns. Reward and satisfaction come as a by-product of addressing the needs of others.

By focusing all your efforts and energy on a particular goal, you can achieve anything. Be sure it is worth it.

If you focus on small goals, you will probably achieve them. If you focus on large goals, and work toward them daily, you will probably achieve them, in addition to all your smaller goals. Watch for distractions and substitutes – they are time wasters. Stay on target and know what you are trying to achieve. Focus can often be undercut by fatigue, lack of fitness and disorganization. You must deal with these underlying issues in order to achieve anything worthwhile.

**Follow-Up**  Follow-up is essential for successful business or personal relations. Check back on everything.

**Food**  Eat only when you are hungry, not just because you feel like it.

**Foolish**  Do not worry about appearing foolish when trying to do something positive.

**Force**  Whatever is done by force is undone by time.

**Forgive** Forgiveness is essential for a happy life. Without it, life narrows to nothing but bitterness.

**Forgot** "Sorry, I forgot" is not an acceptable excuse. You are responsible for remembering. Write everything down if you have to. Do not make false excuses for forgetting.

**Framework** The best operating framework for a leader is summed up with two words: "respect" for and "appreciation" of others.

**Freedom** You are never really free until you are free of the need for the approval of others. Everything starts with our freedom to think. Give others that freedom as well.

**Friends** Making and keeping friends requires a little consideration. Making and keeping enemies requires none. Work on being a friend and you will have some. Good friends help us to avoid rationalizing poor decisions and bad behavior.

**Fun** Have fun.

# G

**Gap**  It is the distance between what is and what can be, or between what people have and what they want. Close the gap.

**Generous**  Be generous in everything. Give more than is asked or expected, in time, attention, caring, empathy and support. Never mind what others will think of you; doing so will have a profound effect on how you think of you.

**Gentleman**  "Gentleman" originally meant a land owner or farmer. Over time it came to mean someone who was courteous, considerate, polite and empathetic. To today's generation it means a "loser," that is, someone who can accept losing, since they probably do so often, or some who fares badly on dates by not being aggressive enough. Aim for the middle definition.

**Geographical Cure**  The problem with continually switching locations or jobs or relationships is that we keep taking ourselves with us. Our choice is to either grow or run.

**Gifted**  Gifted or talented people generally do not have these gifts in all directions. There are blind and even foolish parts to their lives.

**Gifts**  The gift that really counts is the gift of one's self, that is, your time, consideration, empathy, encouragement and love. Everything else is just a substitute.

**Givers**  There are givers and takers in life. Givers add to any given situation or relationship. Takers are generally consumed by self. They detract or take from events and associations. People are always glad to see a giver coming and pleased to see a taker going. It is the givers who have real success in life.

**Giving**  Give more than you get, and give without expecting anything back. You will be surprised with what you get back.

"If you want to be rich, start giving money away." – A. Christ

**Giving Up**  "Never give in. Never give in. Never, never, never ... except to convictions of honor and good sense." – Winston Churchill speaking at Harrow School after the Second World War

**Glory**  In most projects, endeavors or companies, there is glory enough for all but not enough for someone who wants it all. Don't seek it – share it. Build up others. Those who try to grab glory for themselves rarely get any.

**Goals**  Establish achievable goals and write them down. Break goals up into bite-size pieces by amount or time frame, such as daily or weekly objectives. This will help you to work "in the now" versus having some lofty, distant objective. Once you have achieved a goal, set one higher in order to move to the next plateau. Be very careful about completely changing your goals and certainly do not do it very often. It is a tip-off to giving up.

**God**  Most people who have accomplished great things have a faith and accountability beyond themselves. Move in that direction and avoid substitutes, particularly yourself. Look up, not horizontally. Your life is essentially between you and your God.

**Good**  Whenever something challenging or negative arises, state: "That's good." Then try to find out what is good about it. You will find opportunities.

If you want to do good things in life, start with the person next to you or those closest to you.

**Good Day**  Ask yourself each morning: "What do I have to do to have a good day?"

**Good Times**  Often we do not recognize good times until long after they are gone. Try to appreciate everything all the time.

Do not let your overhead creep up too much in good times. The difficult periods will be back.

**Goodwill**  It is always good to build up goodwill, but do not be afraid to draw on it from time to time. That is what it is there for – to be used.

**Gossip**  If you want to hurt a person (and yourself), talk about another person. If you want to help someone, talk to them.

**Grace**  The highest form of compassion is grace. It is kindness and forgiveness when they are not deserved. Most of us need some grace in our lives. Try to provide it to others.

**Gracious**  Be gracious to others in all respects: courtesy, kindness, respect and forgiveness.

**Gratitude**  Practicing gratitude is a great way to overcome depression and negativity. If you do not practice gratitude (saying or thinking "thank you"), it is an easy slide into entitlement. Gratitude is a foundation for happiness. Show your appreciation to others, but do not expect it.

**Gray** There is no gray, just black and white, right and wrong, good and evil. In between is where we rationalize our behavior and the trouble begins.

**Greed** Greed destroys a person's reputation, relationships, values, real potential — and eventually their soul. Greed both creates and reflects problems.

**Greet** Make a point of greeting people. Come out of yourself with a simple smile, "hello" or "good morning." It brightens lives and is, as a result, a success ingredient.

**Group Think** There will always be pressures to think and act in a certain way. Always be open to examining your thinking, but beware of altering your core values of right and wrong on the basis of societal or corporate fads.

**Growing Up** Children blame their parents. Adults thank them.

**Growth**  Growth is usually painful and sometimes frightening. More often than not, we are forced to grow by circumstances. Without growth, nothing really changes. We simply move in and out of the same situations. Internal and external progress go together.

Personal or financial growth results from changes in perceptions, circumstances, events or expectations. Try to discern the possibilities for change, and then act.

**Grudges**  Grudges are for school or prison yards, not business settings.

**Guidance**  Often when a deal or relationship does not work out, it is guidance. Try to think and see things in those terms.

# H

**Habit**  It takes three weeks to learn or unlearn a habit. That's just 21 days.

**Hallucination**  "Imagination without execution is hallucination." – A. S. Fell

**Hanging In**  Hanging in is sometimes winning. If you hang in long enough, you will succeed.

**Happiness**  "Grab every scrap of happiness while you can." – Noël Coward

The key to happiness is low expectations. Try to be grateful for everything that comes your way. Only you can make you happy; no one else can.

**Hard**  Do not avoid the hard things in life, whether they be actions or decisions. Dealing with tough things on a timely basis is reflective of character and leadership potential. It also helps build self-esteem.

**Hardship**  Get the best and the most out of every difficult situation. There should be some reward for enduring hardship.

**Hard Work**  Hard work is no substitute for smart work. Think about what you are doing and always try to find a better way.

**Hate**  On being hated: "Don't give way to hating."
– Rudyard Kipling

**Have**  Instead of being grateful for what they have, many people are obsessed with what they don't have. It is usually good to have goals and desires, but it is always good to know what we have going for us.

**Healing**  Time and healing go together.

**Health**  Good health is always taken for granted, until it is gone. Stay in shape, take care of yourself and be grateful.

**Heart**  Look at a person's heart more than at their actions or words.

**Hell**  "If you are going through hell, keep going." – Winston Churchill

If there is hell, there is heaven.

**Hello**  No one is important enough to justify being aloof. Say "hello" to people. It may help or encourage them in some small way.

**Help**  The only people who can be helped are those who want to be helped. Every time you help someone else, you help yourself. The first question to ask yourself each morning is "How can I help someone today?" A good last question of the day is "Did I help someone today?" Help can be done in any context – whether business or personal.

**Here to There**  When you don't know how to get from here to there, wait for inspiration. For those who can pray, seek God's guidance. Occasionally, talking to others can help, even if you don't take their advice.

**Hide** Don't hide from issues, decisions or new information. Be open and ready to address what needs to be done. People often use pride to hide.

**High Ground** In any battle or contest, it is always important to fight on your terms and on terrain favorable to you. Typically, this means taking and holding the high ground, from which you can look down upon your enemies and force them to attack in a disadvantageous uphill battle. The discipline is in not getting lured or angered into fighting on the enemy's terms or terrain.

Occasionally, taking and holding the high ground entails simply walking away.

**History** Every nation has its own version, and it is very important to each one. Try to understand others' historical views in order to understand their thinking and actions. Most people do not know their own history, just their mythology. We live only in a sliver of time. Try to understand people, events and decisions outside those you are currently experiencing.

**Holidays**  If you don't take holidays, you will get sick. Whether they are short or long, take breaks from your work for the sake of yourself, your family, your fellow employees, your customers and your friends.

**Honesty**  Honesty appears covered when you say: "I told them the details." Rigorous honesty means: "I made sure they understood the key points." Aim for the latter. If you are known to be honest, it will more than make up for your failings. If you are seen as dishonest, it won't matter what your assets are.

**Honors**  They come from doing, not grasping. If you feel unworthy, you are probably the right person to receive honors.

**Hope**  Hope energizes – get some. It is a key ingredient for life and without it we are ready to die.

Work at having hope for the future, for your ideas and for your possibilities. See the positives in the present and their possibilities for the future.

**Hostility**  People watch, so hostility to one is hostility to all. They wonder when their turn will come.

**Hubris**  Just equate this with disaster.

**Humility**  One thing is certain about humility: if you do not practice it, it will be provided for you. Be open to learn and grow. Respect the opinions of others.

**Humor**  Try to keep a sense of humor about yourself and your circumstances. It will help with perspective. Sometimes it takes a real effort, but not taking things too seriously can be an emotional escape valve.

Be careful when you lose your ability to laugh, particularly at yourself. Avoid put-down, racist, sexist or off-color jokes.

**Hurdles**  Focus on the goal, not the hurdles.

**Hurt**  You cannot inflict hurt without experiencing hurt.

**Hurts**  You are not going to get through life without hurts. Try to see them as opportunities to learn and grow. Don't nurse them or rehearse them.

# I

**I** Try to restrict the word "I" to your own personal feelings or opinions. If you are a leader, or wish to be a good one, use the term "we" as much as possible.

**Ideas** People buy into an idea rather than an object. An idea and its allure are what draw people. The idea or underlying benefit is the essence of the reasons for action. Ideas and actions should go together.

**Ideology** Starts with a conclusion. Better is to start with a question.

**If** "If you can keep your head when all about you
    Are losing theirs and blaming it on you,
  If you can, trust yourself when all men doubt
    you,

But make allowance for their doubting too;
If you can, wait and not be tired by waiting,
Or being lied about, don't deal in lies,
Or being hated, don't give way to hating ...
you'll be a Man, my son!"
– Rudyard Kipling, "If"

**Ignorant**  Not knowing a thing is just ignorant. Not wanting to know is stupid. It takes pride to get from one to the other.

**Imagination**  "You cannot tell from appearances how things will go. Sometimes imagination makes things out far worse than they are; yet without imagination not much can be done." – Winston Churchill, speaking at Harrow School, 1941

**Impatience**  Impatience is a two-edged sword that can get things done, but with a cost. It's okay to be impatient about things but not with people.

**Important**  There is not a great deal in life that is truly important, but what is important is usually very important. Determine what is important, then address it and leave the rest.

**Impress** Trying to impress others usually has exactly the opposite effect. Efforts to impress someone can hamper our ability to listen, and compel us to interrupt in order to be noticed. The desire to impress is a symptom of insecurity or low self-esteem. Relax. Be yourself. That's more than enough.

**Indecision** Be very careful about changing your decisions. Usually your first decision is right. Unless you acquire totally new information, changes are often based on fear.

**Indecisive** A fear-based trait. People are not indecisive because they are overworked. They are overworked because they are indecisive.

**Independent** So-called "independent" personalities can be very destructive in achieving a team's goals.

**Indignation**  Some turn this into a way of life. Being indignant does not imply positive corrective action but, rather, nurturing the offense.

**Information**  Information is power. Listen and communicate effectively. Try to discern what is "decisionable" from simple background static.

**Initial Contact**  State who you are, who you represent and the purpose of your call right at the start, then see where it goes from there.

**Injustice**  The world is filled with injustices. The conversations of many people are based on the petty injustices they have suffered at the hands of bosses, spouses, bank tellers, store clerks, etc. This is not only boring and negative, but also a major energy drain. The only way to get out of this rut and deal with injustice is through forgiveness, although often undeserved.

**Innovative**  Always be looking for a better way of doing things. Hard work is no substitute for smart work.

**Insanity** It is like a black hole, sucking everything and everyone into it. Whenever you have one person behaving in a bizarre manner, you can guarantee that behavior will spread.

Emotionally detach as best you can, or you too will become part of the problem.

**Inspire** Aspire to inspire before you expire.

**Instincts** Trust them. They are often our experiences nudging us. "Gut feel" tends to become more reliable with age.

**Instruction** Instruction, if it is to be beneficial, should never descend into criticism.

**Integrity** Integrity is continuously trying to do the right thing for the right reasons. Integrity is the passport to get you where you want to be in life. It also implies self-examination and empathy for others.

**Interrupt** Never interrupt. Always give the other person the opportunity to concentrate and fully articulate their ideas. Disrespectful interruptions frustrate and alienate.

**Interview** The real job or prospect interview begins before the face-to-face meeting. Did you follow up with a telephone call or call back when you said you would? Were you there on time (i.e., ten minutes early)? Did you send any additional material to the interviewer as promised? Did you show gratitude for having the meeting? The list goes on. You are judged before you even show up, as well as afterward.

**Interviewing the Prospect to Be a Customer** Remember, there are some customers or clients you *don't* want. When interviewing someone to be a customer, you are also interviewing them for an ongoing business relationship.

**Intolerance** The new face of intolerance is political correctness.

**Introspection** Review your thinking and behavior against results. Then correct those traits that sabotage success, relationships and self-worth. This process requires rigorous and fearless self-honesty.

**Intuition** "A woman's guess is usually more accurate than a man's certainty." – Rudyard Kipling
Never underestimate a woman's intuition.

**Inventory** From time to time, take an inventory of yourself – write down what you consider to be your assets and your liabilities. Look at why you do things. Examine selfishness, greed, self-will, habits, situations, relationships, etc. Don't beat yourself up (there are always others available to do that), but try to be objective in order to spot areas for improvement.

**Invest** Invest in yourself, your business and your career. Take courses, go to seminars, spend time building your knowledge. Your investment in yourself also includes your appearance, business attire and support items such as a reasonable car, which is kept clean.

**Irreplaceable**  In order to be irreplaceable, one must be different.

**Isolate**  Do not isolate yourself from others. We all need a sense of association and belonging. If you are part of a family, stay part of it. That is how we grow and mature.

People can be infuriating; that is why we need to associate with others – to deal with our being infuriated.

**Issues**  People with issues rarely think they have them. Only the pain of living can give clarity, not the efforts of others to point them out.

If you do not deal with your issues, they will deal with you.

# J

**Jealousy** An absolutely useless and destructive human trait. Instead of looking horizontally, strive to look up with gratitude and see the possibilities.

**Job** If you do not see your job as important, people won't see you as important. There are more good jobs than there are good people to fill them. Attitude, skills and experience must be packaged and presented or "sold" to the real decision makers in order to land the position you should have.

**Journey** We are all on a journey without the certainty of arriving. Enjoy the journey as best you can, and as you look back you will find that even the dead ends were not wastes of time. Pressing on and doing your best, one day at a time, will lead you to a place of victory, even if it was not your original goal. We often set our sights too low.

**Joy** When you lose your joy, everything becomes a major chore. Try to be joyful about life in general and yours in particular. A sense of fun is part of this. You get joy by giving it.

**Judging** "Judge not that you not be judged." Be careful when you open up the judging game, since you will probably be included. Judging is a form of condemning others that caters to our egos.

**Judgment** Good judgment comes from experience, and experience comes from bad judgment. Don't beat yourself up too much. We are all learning.

**Justice** Most of us demand justice when we should be seeking mercy or grace. You can demand justice but not generosity.

**Justify** Do a thing because it is right or good, not because you have cast a person or group as evil.

# K

**Kind**  Being kind is one of the best investments you can make. It bears great dividends and is infectious. Take the time to be kind to others; the world will appear to be a better place.

**Knowledge**  The most important things in life are what you learn after you know everything.

# L

**Lack**  What you lack can fuel your drive to accomplish and succeed. Use what you do not have as an asset.

**Language**  Work hard to speak well. If English is your second language, work at pronunciation as well as grammar. If people have to strain to listen, they will stop listening.

**Late**  Leaders are never late. Ever. A leader being continually late diminishes the people working for them and the tasks they are performing.

Continual lateness is arrogance in action and a defect of character. It also undercuts confidence. Early is good.

**Laugh**  Laugh at yourself and your circumstances as often as you can. It shows you are not taking either too seriously, and it is a sign of good mental health.

**Lawsuits**  An old Gypsy curse: "May you be involved in a lawsuit in which you know you are right." Avoid lawsuits as much as possible, and try to settle whenever possible.

**Lazy**  Laziness leads directly to sloppiness and unreliability. The problem is that no one sees themselves as being any of these. Rigorous self-examination is hard for anyone, let alone someone who is lazy.

**Leaders**  Great leaders are more concerned about the importance of others than of themselves.

**Leadership**  Leadership is essentially sacrificial. This is not taught in business schools, only in church and in the military. Good leaders take care of the people in their charge, ahead of themselves. If the people under you trust and have confidence in you, the people above you will as well.

Controlling one's emotions and remaining cool in all circumstances also set a good leader apart.

Individuals who try to use an organization to build themselves up are generally leadership disasters.

Leadership is, in part, an exercise in faith. A true leader works on the basis that his or her success is dependent on the success of the whole enterprise.

**Learn**  We learn by listening, seeing or experiencing. Sadly, most of us have to experience a thing first-hand in order to learn. Experience is generally the most painful way to learn, but certainly the most effective – if we survive. A basic choice in life is learn or argue. One excludes the other.

People generally have to learn the important things from their own pain.

**Leisure**  This is not an "at your leisure" world. We are all in some form of competition.

**Lend** Never lend; give. You will keep more friends as well as be of real help. Giving cuts your loan-loss exposure.

**Lesser Fears** Confront your lesser fears or your larger fears will overtake you.

**Liabilities** Do not acquire liabilities and call them assets.

**Life** Life is a "come as you are" affair, but it is not a "stay as you are" affair. Get on with it. Try to improve and deal with things as you go.

Life should not be a zero-sum affair. Richness comes from what you add to it.

"Love your life." – Written on a child's T-shirt. A great sentiment and guideline for all of us.

**Limit** Many entrepreneurs limit the growth of their organizations by being unable or unwilling to move out of their comfort zones. When longer-term growth stalls, either thinking or management should change. This holds for individuals as well.

Do not put limits on yourself in terms of what you can accomplish, and don't limit your success by settling for too little.

**Listen** Don't shut off inputs by talking too much. Listen to both what is said and what is not. Remember, what people say and what they are telling you are often quite different. Show that you are interested. Listen with your whole body.

We generally listen to what we want to hear. We should try to listen to what we don't want to hear.

**Loan** Think of all your gifts, skills, talents, relationships, looks, health and possessions as simply being on loan. They will all go at some point, so enjoy and appreciate them and use them wisely.

**Lofty Ideals** They mean little if not underpinned by personal behavior such as integrity and kindness.

**Lonesome**  You are never really alone.

**Long-Term Goals**  They are fine to have, but keep in mind that they can be an excellent source of procrastination, since the key phrase is "long-term." More critical is one's daily effort. Daily objectives are the real building blocks of success.

**Loser**  Being a loser is a personal decision that only you can make.

**Love**  Love is the only thing that really matters, that is, caring for and about others. Everything else in life is just an "add on." Love begets love. There is an unending supply, with more than enough to go around.

True love does not require a response.

**Loyalty**  It is not a dated concept. If you expect loyalty, you must give it. Organizations that demand it up the line, yet never give it down the line, are ongoing disasters in terms of morale.

Be loyal, fair, supportive and considerate to people and they will more than reciprocate in kind. Loyalty has a cost, but it also pays substantial dividends in terms of long-term friendships and associations.

Loyalty is also standing up for others and for what is right. Gratitude is optional. Loyalty is not.

**Lucky**  When asked who his favorite generals were, Napoleon answered: "The lucky ones."

If you are continually "unlucky," some thinking or changing might be in order.

# M

**Management**  Not to be confused with leadership. Management is "how to." Leadership is "why to."

Management is essentially sales. It is about understanding people's needs and fears, and then selling them on the tasks at hand and on how the organization can meet their goals. All of this must be done subtly; being too overt undercuts credibility. Watch carefully for signs of unmet needs, and address them if you wish to keep your team together.

**Management Teams**  Within the team, and probably within the whole organization, "everyone is responsible for everything," as all tasks are interrelated and the goal is to help one another.

**Managing**  One of the dangers in managing is over-managing. Give clear instructions, mandates, information, etc., and then get out of the way. Let people do their work and use their brains. Managers can fool themselves into thinking they are being productive when in fact they are slowing things down or interfering.

**Marriage**  Marriage is similar to a corporate merger. To be successful, one plus one should equal more than two.

The payback in effort, patience and sacrifice is well worth it in the strength, encouragement and meaning that come from a successful marriage.

**Material Wealth**  It is not to be diminished or unappreciated, but when someone dies and the question "How much money did they leave?" arises, the answer is always the same: "All of it!" The real thing we leave (and possibly take) is how we touched others.

**Maturity**  Maturity is having made the journey from self to others.

**Meaning**  Find out what gives real meaning to your life, then do it – now.

**Means**  "The means you choose determine the ends you get." – A. Griffin

**Media**  Typically, one does not earn most of the positive press one gets. The same is true of negative press.

**Mediocre**  There is no reason for being mediocre, just excuses.

**Meetings**  When organizing a meeting, ask yourself if it is really necessary and what you want to achieve. Have a clear agenda and fixed start and finish times. Keep it brief and to the point.

Stay focused on your goal and work toward it in a straight line, as much as that is possible. Do not let others drag you all over the verbal countryside with side issues. Yes, address concerns, but stay on target. Control the agenda and your presentation.

**Memories**  All we really leave at the end of our journey is memories. Try to make them good ones.

**Memos**  Virtually all the memos ever written can be boiled down to "Use your brain."

**Menial Jobs**  What some see as menial jobs, others see as opportunities. Virtually everyone coming to this country started at a menial job and individually and collectively built something great.

**Message**  Get the message, not the messenger, otherwise the message will get you. Important information is often provided by flawed people. Do not focus on the messenger; try to understand what you are really being told. If you do not, you will experience the full impact of your mistakes.

**Messes**  Most messes are messages. They are telling you something.

**Micro**  People often stay focused on micro-issues because they are easier to deal with. It is a form of procrastination.

**Mind Lock**  The inability to question one's views, attitudes and behaviors is a major cause of disappointment and failure. Be open to new information, insights and opinions. Remain curious.

**Minor Details**  People often get caught up in micro-issues when they have lost either their big-picture view or their confidence. Ask: "How important is it?"

Some years ago, an airplane crashed in the Everglades because the flight crew focused on a minor instrument problem, rather than the direction of the aircraft.

**Miracles**  "Anyone who doesn't believe in miracles is not a realist." – David Ben-Gurion

**Miserable**  Miserable people want to make everyone else miserable. You can substitute here the word "negative" or even "happy" for "miserable."

**Mistakes**  Everyone makes mistakes. Don't be afraid to admit them. It will show strength and confidence. Attempt to learn from them, and try not to beat yourself up over them. Keep your perspective and your sense of humor, and then move on, a little wiser for the experience.

**Moderation**  Avoid extremes and live moderately.

**Money**  Money should be a servant to do good or to help others. It should not be used to intimidate or to show off. Money is often an index of service to others. Money cannot buy love.

**Mood**  Do not let your mood affect your thinking, actions, relationships and, most of all, reputation. If you are going through a period of depression, anger or fear, just "lay low." Do not make key decisions, engage in serious or combative discussions or show your mental state.

**Morals**  Having morals is striving to be accountable to a higher standard of behavior.

**Motivate**  Try to understand what motivates people (and yourself). Everyone is influenced by a series of needs and desires, but typically there is a dominant one. When you grasp that one, you will know how an individual thinks and how to deal with them.

**Motivation**  Motivation is the desire for, and commitment to, your own success. In action, it shows up as the determination to go the distance, do what is necessary, stay committed, get better, plug energy leaks, get rid of bad habits and see yourself as successful.

**Motives**  Watch for good motives covering bad motives, particularly when you are offering criticism or advice. People know when you are "for" them and when you are not. If you are truly striving to be of service or to be helpful, people generally recognize and appreciate it.

**Move**  Keep moving until you can't.

**Multimillionaire**  If you want to live like a multi-millionaire, you probably should be one.

**Multiplier**  The actions and emotions of a leader are multiplied in intensity by those who are following. Stay calm and level.

# N

**Names**  Never diminish a person by calling them a name – even in traffic. It diminishes you.

**Needs**  If you focus on the needs of others, yours will be met.

Try to separate your needs from your wants. It helps one to concentrate on what is important.

**Needy**  People who need to be liked, loved or admired tend to become glory grabbers and attention seekers. In so doing, they usually destroy the chances of success in any area.

**Negative People**  Avoid them.

**Negatives** Focusing on negatives is a great destroyer. Social media, TV and the Internet are a rich source of negatives. You can't accomplish very much by seeking, concentrating on or stressing negatives. Being negative is a choice that develops into a habit. Only you can change that downward spiral.

**Negotiations** Negotiations can be used to gain insight into how the other party thinks. This perspective is very important when a longer-term relationship is being contemplated.

**Networking** Relationship building is generally more productive than networking. It involves greater focus and finesse.

**News** Do you want to watch it or make it?

**Next Level** What do you have to do to get there?

**No** It is not the answer "no" that will lead to failure. It is accepting "maybe." Do not be afraid of clear direction. Be afraid of wasting time.

**Nothing**  If you do nothing, you get nothing. This also holds for half-baked efforts. "Nothing for nothing" is a phrase to remember.

**Now**  Do it now. Do not let the tasks necessary for success pile up. Get on with them and avoid procrastination. Put in extra hours to get caught up if necessary, then move forward.

# O

**Objectivity** If you lose objectivity, you lose credibility.

**Obligations** It is up to you to remind yourself of your obligations, not others.

**Observe** Develop the skill of observing people, that is, how they act, react, speak and even see themselves. With practice, you will be able to anticipate their behavior and see where your relationships with them will lead, if emotions don't blind you.

**Obstacles** Don't build them up; tear them down, both mentally and physically.

**Offense** Do not spend time taking offense. If you look for offense, you will find it.

**Old Age** It is a bad habit that busy people do not have the time to fall into. If you lose your reason for living, you lose your will for living. Stay involved, relevant, curious and working.

**Once** Touch papers on your desk only once. Do not examine them and stack them up for later action. Deal with them immediately. Forward them and attach notes or throw them out.

Keep the deck clear for action. Treat mini-items coming across your desk like hot potatoes – spend no time handling them. Get rid of them with a quick decision.

**One Day at a Time** Fight your battles in day-tight compartments. Don't look too far back or too far forward. Do your best each day. Review each day to see if what you have done has moved you closer to your goals. If not, try to do better the next day.

Occasionally, when you are under stress, you may be able to function only one hour or even just ten minutes at a time. Just keep inching forward without the baggage from the past or the anxieties of the future.

**100 Percent** Be a "100 percenter" 100 percent of the time. Ninety percent is great in school, but disastrous in most other activities.

**Opinion** Your opinion is not as important as someone's feelings. If you must give an opinion, do it with kindness and compassion. People always remember how you make them feel.

Opinions are not necessarily reality, so do not carve them in stone.

**Opportunities** They are often about perception, that is, seeing something others do not, then acting.

**Opportunity** Each day, look at your biggest challenge — for example, procrastination, distractions, energy drains or emotions. Then try to see what your greatest opportunity is. Focus your efforts on the latter. Long-term goals are great, but the daily exercise of working on your greatest opportunity is absolutely necessary in order to achieve your long-term goals.

**Optimism**  If you are alive, you have no grounds for anything but optimism.

**Order**  Without a sense of order, chaos becomes the norm. All endeavors require both a functioning framework and a degree of accountability.

**Organization**  Being organized is central to building relationships. People who fail to follow through on their commitments are often seen as dishonest, unreliable or uncaring. In many cases, they are simply disorganized.

Note all your commitments and the requests or wishes of your friends or customers. You will be amazed at the surprise and appreciation of others when you deliver the goods, even when the request or commitment was simply a passing comment.

Being organized will build your reputation as being reliable and considerate.

**Others** Putting others first will inspire those around you, and establish your leadership. Leadership is about others. Maturing is making the journey from "self" to "others."

**Outflow** If your financial outflow is greater than your income, your upkeep will be your downfall. Live within your means and build. Stretching yourself can be good, but catch up on a regular basis.

**Out of Control** A leader must never be seen as being out of control. Whenever it happens, those being led will start thinking about alternatives. People want to feel emotionally secure, whether that be with their jobs, relationships or investments.

**Overcoming** Life is a business of overcoming events, things and ourselves. Understanding this is important for both personal progress and endurance.

**Overreaction**  Everyone has overreacted at some point. It is, however, just an attention-getting device with no real positive result.

**Overworked**  Overworked and underorganized are often the same thing. Prioritize.

# P

**Packaging** Consider how you package yourself and your product. Dress, manner of speech and attitude are all part of your packaging.

**Pain** One cannot get through life without pain. Often those who have suffered are the ones with the greatest compassion for others; possibly that is one of the reasons for it. If you are suffering through pain, try to find the gain in it. Look for a positive or opportunity to offset your suffering.

**Panic** "You, you and you panic. The rest, follow me." – A sergeant dealing with a tough situation
  You can decide which group you belong to.

**Parenting**   Style is important but outcome is more important. Rules are good but unconditional love is essential.

**Participate**   Get involved. Do not be a bench-warmer through life.

**Part-Timers**   Never be a part-timer. Be fully involved and committed, otherwise you will miss what is going on or miss the steps necessary for success.

**Passengers**   "There are no passengers on earth. We are all crew." – Marshall McLuhan

**Passion**   Passion comes from strong beliefs coupled with courage. Generally, people prefer passion over coldness, as long as it carries respect for others and their views.

Be passionate about what you do and you will be successful.

**Passive Aggressive**  There is no room for this type of behavior in an adult business environment or adult relationship. People who take out their emotional issues on others by being obstructionists should be sidelined or simply removed. They drain others and can seriously undercut positive initiatives.

**Past**  Many appraisals, decisions and actions are based on history, rather than on the future. Although the past is an important tool, include "what can be" in your thought processes. Future possibilities are the keys to progress. Have a vision.

Don't drag past hurts around with you like Jacob Marley's chains. Move forward from today, unburdened.

**Pathological**  People who are pathological always blame others for their reactions to their own bad behavior. Often this shows in just small ways at first, but the trait becomes more pronounced as the individual continues to push the boundaries. The earlier this highly destructive behavior is removed, the better.

**Patience** There is a time to "let go and let God." This is very hard for most people. After you have done your very best, back off and let the weight of your efforts sink in.

**Pattern** Is there a pattern or trend in your life? Only you are responsible.

**Payments** The best time to start paying for something is before you buy it. Develop the habit of saving and investment.

**Peace** Peace and forgiveness go together.

**People** People will let you down, consciously or unconsciously. They are weak and fallible and are affected by fear, pride, anger, prejudice, frustration and ambition.

Accepting this fact, and the fact that you too share some of those traits, will enable you to go forward, with some degree of understanding and forgiveness. This will also enable you to be realistic in your expectations of and demands on others.

Do not waste time, energy or focus on people who are not prepared to put effort into a relationship with you.

**Perception**  Perception is usually affected by our perspective. Try to see things as they really are. Therein lies the possibility of improvement.

**Perfect**  Nothing and no one is perfect. We have a choice of what we will focus on.

**Perfectionists**  There are no happy perfectionists.

**Performance**  Does your performance match the goals you have established?

**Perfunctory**  Do not be perfunctory in anything you do.

**Permanent**  More often than not, what appears permanent is simply a passing phase.

**Permit**  What we permit we promote.

**Perseverance**  Vince Lombardi, the legendary football coach, claimed that there wasn't a game his team could not have won, if the game had gone on long enough. He referred to stamina and determination as character in action. They are needed in order to stick to the tasks required for success, particularly in adverse conditions.

**Persistence**  Persistence is often more important than "smarts." Consistency of effort is essential to achieving any goal. People who continually shift their focus and efforts have a tendency to stay in one place.

**Persona**  We each create our own persona, and we are the only ones who can change it.

**Personal Attacks**  You won't get far in business or life without coming under some personal attacks.

The best defense in those times is self-esteem, and that comes from trying to do the right thing. Knowing who you are and standing on your own integrity are critical in working through those periods.

**Personal Business**  If you start your business day with personal matters, you will probably find that the day is substantially wasted in terms of business achievement. Try to schedule those tasks for the end of the day, after you have accomplished something.

**Personal Freedom**  To be free from negativity, we must work our way through the doorway of anger and move down the hallway of acceptance in order to arrive at the living room of forgiveness. That's a faith journey, and forgiveness is the destination.

**Personality Types**  There are "can do," "can't do" and "won't do" people in all walks of life. Though they do not make a conscious decision to be in the latter two categories, many people are. Look at yourself honestly and decide to be in the first category – "can do" – then work at it each and every day.

Do not spend a great deal of time trying to work with "can't do" and "won't do" types.

**Perspective**  It is very easy to lose your bearings during times of trial. Focus on what is important, good or right at these moments. Try to be grateful for something.

**Pettiness**  Don't major in the minors. Get on with the bigger things.

**Physical**  Do not let your physical blessings fuel any sense of superiority or arrogance. Those attributes can be liabilities if they define how you think of yourself. It is the people who fight to overcome some perceived disadvantage who generally succeed in life.

**Plan**  Plan your work and work your plan.

**Plan A** Plan A will probably not work. Success comes from working with Plans B, C, D or E.

**Planning** As any carpenter will tell you, measure twice and cut once. Vision requires a plan.

**Playground** Consider life as a playground. Try to have fun and play nicely with the other children.

**Pleasant** "I have discovered in life you have to be oh so smart or oh so pleasant. I have decided to be oh so pleasant." – James Stewart's character Mr. Dowd in *Harvey*.

It is also true in real life.

**Please** "Please" and "thank you" are probably the most important words in the English language. They show people that they and their actions are appreciated. Not using them will cut you off from others and opportunities.

**Polite** There is only upside to being polite, courteous and considerate.

**Political Correctness**  It is a pale and sometimes tyrannical substitute for decency.

**Poor Choices**  There is always a cost to poor choices, and we are always surprised at the size of the bill. These are conscious decisions we know are not right, but we continue to make them — for example, cutting corners, forgetting integrity and honesty, smoking, bad attitudes, substance abuse or simply overeating.

**Popularity**  If everyone likes you, you are doing something wrong.

**Positive:Negative Ratio**  Always keep your positive comments and ideas ahead of the negatives. Be known as a realistically positive, "can do" type of person, as opposed to being a negative faultfinder. Don't justify negatives on the basis of being realistic or helpful.

**Possessions**  Possessions can possess us with their demands for time and attention. Travel light.

**Possibilities** Look for the possibilities in all that is presented to you, and especially in the negatives. This will separate you from those who grasp only the obvious. Possibilities are not limited by your past or present circumstances.

**Potential** You will not know your real potential until you get moving. If you have the humility to learn, you will expand that potential. Also, a key task of any great leader is helping others realize their own greatest potential.

**Power** Personal power comes from the alignment of positive values and actions.

**Prayer** Ask for help in the morning and give thanks at the end of the day. Even if you are not a believer, it will help with perspective and gratitude.

**Preparation** Lack of preparation undercuts confidence and the chances of success.

**Pressure** Do not respond to pressure tactics. Try not to inflict pressure on others by using artificial time limits or the possibility of dire consequences. Lay out the facts truthfully. The difference between enthusiasm and pressure is that one is attractive and the other self-promoting. One fosters empathy; the other, hostility.

**Pretend**   Do not pretend to be someone's friend if you are not. Asking "How are you today?" when introducing yourself may be seen as hypocritical. You likely don't really care, and the prospect knows that. It is a poor start to a potentially productive relationship.

**Pride**   Pride is often used to cover feelings of insecurity or inadequacy. You can afford to be compassionate with prideful people.

**Priorities**   There should be a connection between potential and time commitments. Take a moment to attempt to discern proper priorities before leaping into action.

**Prison**   Without forgiveness, you condemn yourself to an emotional prison.

**Problems** Anybody can deal with one problem at a time. It's when you have four or five simultaneously that discouragement can set in. Remember, if any one of them can't destroy you, the sum total can't bury you. Break them down into simple challenges and try to deal with each one separately, even if you have to assign specific times or days to deal with each.

What most people think are problems are really symptoms. For example, money problems rarely exist, except for counterfeiters. Money symptoms are the norm, as they simply reflect the real underlying problem(s). Find out what the real problem is, deal with it and watch the symptom evaporate.

Any problem that money can solve is not a real problem.

**Procrastination** Most of us will use pride, fear, illness, fatigue, time of day, anger, resentment, etc. – often negative emotions or thoughts – to avoid doing the "do" things. The basis of procrastination is often the fear of rejection. One of the best ways to overcome it is to become enthusiastic about something and try to get into action. Confidence and self-esteem will follow. Careers, marriages and businesses often fail as a result of procrastination.

**Product**  You are your product. How are you marketing you?

**Profanity**  Try to avoid any and all profanity. Keep your standards high. Many people remove themselves from serious consideration by trying to emphasize a point or describe a characteristic in an offensive manner.

**Programming**  Do not program yourself for defeat by accepting or rehearsing negatives about yourself. Listen, grow and change, then move on.

"Whatever you say after 'I am' is going to come looking for you." – Joel Osteen

**Progress**  Very often, progress is measured in inches. Do not be discouraged. As you look back, you will see the great distance you have traveled.

Do not be upset by the seemingly greater progress of others. Your direction is what is important. You may catch them as they plateau or decline, or as you have spurts of growth, or possibly not at all. Your journey is what counts. Look up instead of sideways.

**Projection**   Be careful when you ascribe your feelings to others. That is typically a distress reaction and usually wrong.

**Promises**   Promises must be kept. Be careful and realistic when making them. If there is any uncontrollable change, let the other party know as soon as possible and seek a joint solution. A promise can be made only when there cannot be unforeseen circumstances – therefore, use them advisedly.

"A promise made is a debt unpaid." – Robert W. Service, *The Cremation of Sam McGee*

**Prospects**   Everyone is a potential prospect. Just take time out to be a person versus consistently being promotive.

**Prosperity** People who cannot handle prosperity are often sent back to the school of poverty to relearn some basic lessons.

**Punctuality** Always arrive ten minutes early. Being late tells others how unimportant you think them to be. It is also discourteous and irritating to someone who has scheduled time for you. Plan ahead. Consider weather, traffic and other contingencies. Always telephone if you are going to be unavoidably delayed.

**Purpose** You have to have a purpose for your life. You are not here just to hang around. Purpose is essential for self-esteem.

It is a good idea to have a one-sentence "purpose statement" for yourself outlining what you aspire to be and do.

Purpose should precede function. The first questions should be "What are you going to do and why?" The "how" part comes later.

**Put Downs**  You cannot berate people into being successful. Negatives breed negatives. Build on people's assets rather than on their shortcomings.

# Q

**Quality**  Quality means detail. It is the result of continually looking for small ways to be a little better, as well as for ways to be a lot better. This is true for products, companies and individuals. Quality and consistency go together.

**Quest**  Consider your life a quest to do or achieve something great and meaningful.

# R

**Random Walk** Life is not a random walk – things rarely just happen. There are choices and consequences, causes and effects. Look at what is happening in your life and try to see your role in their occurrences. With awareness comes the responsibility for change.

**Rationalizers** Crooks are not as dangerous as rationalizers. Crooks are easier to spot. Rationalizers look like us, sound like us and are us. Never rationalize bad behavior.

**Read** Language and ideas are connected. Reading improves both speech and the ability to grasp concepts. Read as much as you can, focusing on non-fiction. Draw information and inspiration from historic events and real people. You will find similarities in your own adventures.

**Real**  Be real; that is, what you see is what you get.

**Reality**  It has a way of seeking you out. Address the real issues in life and business, not the substitutes.

**Reasons**  There are always lots of good reasons for bad decisions. There are people who find reasons to act and those who find reasons not to. The latter group usually ends up blaming people, places and things for their failures.

**Reciprocity**  Your attitude and behavior toward others (and those witnessing either) will determine how others respond to you. In the latter instances, the reaction will spread beyond the individuals involved as they talk with friends and acquaintances. Consider the reciprocity factor in all your dealings.

**Recognition** It is a poor substitute for meaning. If one has meaning (purpose) in one's life, recognition often follows.

**Recognize** Recognize mistakes for what they are. Justifying or rationalizing them will stop learning and personal growth. It will also ensure you keep making similar mistakes. Recognizing them also helps in cleaning them up.

**R.E.D.** Rest, Exercise and Diet are important for success. Don't ignore any one of these.

**Regret** It is a good thing, as it points to change.

**Regrets** Most regrets are about things not attempted. Try to cut those down as you go.

People who say they have no regrets are either lying or haven't lived a life.

**Rejection** Rejection is part of the cost of success. Dealing with rejection and still moving forward is what legends are made of.

**Relationships** They are good indicators of success. They are built on trust, respect and consideration. Money is important, but make sure your success is broadly based in the interpersonal sense. Work on building positive relationships; they pay real dividends.

**Relativism** This is one of the many things that must be unlearned after academe. To be successful in life and business, calibrate your behavior in absolutes: black/white, good/evil, right/wrong. Striving to think and live on that basis will help us avoid those gray areas wherein we rationalize our desires, goals and actions, and where real problems develop.

**Relevant** Relationships are based upon being relevant in others' lives. That means you must add something, which requires consideration and effort.

**Remember** Do not forget those who have helped you along the way, even if just in a small way.

**Repentance**  There can be no redemption without repentance. There can also be no reconciliation without repentance. These words are not often used now, but the message is still valid.

**Reputation**  Your reputation will determine whether others want to deal with or be associated with you. It is based upon your word, your actions and your integrity. Never try to build your own reputation by diminishing others.

**Resentment**  This is a killer, and that is not an overstatement. Hanging on to old hurts can virtually destroy people and everything around them as their lives become dominated by bitterness. Fear, anger and resentment are tied together by time. Fear is about the future – "I may not get what I want." Anger concerns the present – "I am not getting what I want." Resentment relates to the past – "I didn't get what I wanted."

Pray for the people you resent, and you'll be amazed at how this destructive feeling evaporates.

"Resentment is like drinking poison and hoping it will kill your enemy." – Nelson Mandela

**Resign** If you resign from life, people will accept your resignation and distance themselves from you. Be involved.

**Resolutions** Do not make New Year's resolutions. Make daily resolves. Long-term intentions do not provide much in the way of guidance for action. The commitment to do something today does. It is the buildup of positive and constructive daily actions that leads to long-term results.

**Respect** The essential glue that holds any organization or relationship together. Without respect, disintegration is a certainty.

If you don't give it, you don't get it. You cannot command it. You must earn it through your actions. Have respect for yourself and for others.

**Responsibilities** Instead of demanding your rights, demand you live up to your responsibilities.

**Responsibility** You are responsible for you – no one else. As soon as we stop blaming people, places or circumstances, we can get to work on ourselves and the things we wish to accomplish.

Leadership is about accepting responsibility, especially when things do not work out.

**Restart** There will be times in business and life when you are slammed down so hard that your energy, optimism and confidence evaporate. People will offer many "dust yourself off" clichés, which, although you may appreciate, simply can't get you going again. Recognize that there are natural mourning and analysis periods, but these should be neither anger nor "wallow" periods. As soon as the event has been digested and understood, try to become positive about yourself, your skills and your prospects. Dig deep into who you are and into your basic desire to be a positive contributor in business and life. As you get back into action, your enthusiasm will return.

**Restraint**  Nothing pays off like restraint of pen and tongue – including emails. This is particularly true when emotions are running high.

**Results**  Results come from combining ability with discipline and drive. The bonding agent is the desire to succeed.

Too often, truly talented people fall by the wayside because of their inability or unwillingness to progress by working hard and smart. Business results come from doing a thing well and letting people know.

If your vision and results are not lining up, examine your thinking and actions.

**Retire**  Never retire. Always be involved, even if it is only a few days each week or as a volunteer. You have to be active and connected with people. Someone once said, "Don't retire, re-fire."

**Retreat**  It is very hard to attack when you are retreating. Establish a point where you will stand, fight and renew the attack. Do not accept continuing setbacks as your lot in life. Often they happen because we allow them to or give them too great a priority in our thinking.

**Revenge**  If you seek revenge, first dig two graves. Forgiveness beats revenge every time.

**Review**  Take the time to compare your goals and your efforts to see if they match. Your daily work should not be considered finished until you have re-examined your efforts and accomplishments.

You may wish to build your own checklist. Whatever form it takes, do it on a regular basis. Do your own time-and-motion study. Are you functioning efficiently?

**Rich**  If you want to be rich, start by giving money away. Don't confuse being rich with being smart.

**Right**  It is not who is right, but what is right. There is no loss of face in changing one's view when confronted with irrefutable facts that show a position to be wrong or flawed. If anything, it shows strength. It is good to be right, but having to be right can be disastrous. Having to be right is a sign of desperation.

**Right Thing**  Do the right thing and things will eventually work out. When there are degrees of right, consider reasonableness.

**Risk**  If you continually bet on 50–50 odds, it is a mathematical certainty that you will go bankrupt. Risks must be taken from time to time, but try to cut the odds against you. Ensure the rewards are commensurate with the risk you are taking. Risks are part of life.

**Rubbish**  Be careful when half your brain manufactures rubbish and the other half buys it.

**Rules**  Rules are made for the many because of the few. Abide by them; don't bend them, ignore them or try to find a way around them. Be strict in your adherence to them.

# S

**Sabotage** Don't worry about external enemies. Your main threat is riding around within you. Many people, particularly talented ones, are so afraid of failing that they never really try anything. This is self-sabotage. They would rather have the fantasy of success than the possible reality of mediocrity, or direction toward another area.

**Sales** The effective communication of an idea or concept in order to influence actions and events. Everything comes down to sales. This holds for life in general, as well as for business.

**Same** Nothing stays the same, but watch for similarities.

**Savings** Make a habit of regularly putting some funds aside. Having some money available will help you to think and function more effectively.

**Say** Say what you do and do what you say. This is a key ingredient for success.

If there is a lot that can be said, it is often better to say nothing.

**Scary** We have scary days to better live the ones we have left.

**Scrooge** In *A Christmas Carol*, Dickens is really illustrating the transition from selfish to selfless. Money and Scrooge's tightness were merely symptoms.

**Second Effort** Sometimes you have to make a second effort many times.

**Security** We all seek security in life and business. Just accept and live with the fact that you will never quite get there. It is often what drives us on.

**See** Try to see what others do not.

**Selective** "Most people put average effort into too many things, rather than superior thought and effort into a few important things. People who achieve the most are selective as well as determined."
– Richard Koch

**Selective Memory** If you are going to remember slights or hurts, try to recall the whole picture, which includes your part in what occurred.

**Self** Self is not a good starting point for leadership.

**Self-Absorbed** Behind many self-absorbed individuals is a spoiled child with a sense of entitlement. Sadly, this has become a metaphor for what our society has become.

**Self-Defense** In times of crisis, we very often imagine the worst-case scenario. This is a self-defense mechanism whereby we prepare ourselves mentally for a complete disaster. The problem is that it programs us to be negative and limits our ability to see the possibilities and to then act constructively.

**Self-Esteem**  Real self-esteem comes through accomplishment, not the affirmation of others.

**Self-Image**  A positive self-image results from, and is affected by, the things we do or don't do. In this regard, responsible or considerate actions, which may not even lead to profit or gain, help us as much as anything. If you envision yourself as successful, the negatives will be seen simply as irritants or material for your autobiography.

A positive self-image is a key ingredient to expecting and demanding success and to overcoming adversity. Do not hang onto things that undermine your self-image, such as bad habits, beat-up cars or wornout clothes.

**Self-Interest**  Bury it helping others. You will be taken care of.

**Self-Justification** This shuts off constructive inputs. Try to substitute self-examination. You will end up with more friends.

We often try to protect our self-image with self-justification. To do otherwise takes courage.

**Self-Pity** Self-pity is both unproductive and unattractive. Dust yourself off and move on.

**Self-Restraint** Practice self-restraint. Without it we will be haunted with regrets.

**Serious** Do not take yourself or circumstances too seriously; you will lose perspective. Just because a situation is serious, it doesn't mean you have to be.

**Sermon** "I would rather see a sermon than hear one any day." – Edgar A. Guest

**Setbacks** They make us stronger. They force us to review, learn, change, grow and overcome. All major successes appear to come out of setbacks and difficulties. They give birth to the determination to persevere. Any fool can benefit from success, but great men are blessed through their setbacks.

**Share**  Share glory, time, finances, everything. You are not taking anything with you.

**Shortcomings**  Get going with what you have and who you are. Try to improve as you move forward. Don't spend too much time fretting about your shortcomings or negatives.

**Shouting**  If you shout, you lose.

**Show Up**  Success is often based on simply showing up. You don't have to run yourself ragged going to every event, but find reasons to show up rather than not. You'll be surprised how opportunities then pop up. Show up and follow up.

**Significant**  Successful and significant are not necessarily connected. Significance comes from helping others to become successful.

**Silence**  Silence is important, as it allows others to assist you with information. You know what you know; find out what someone else knows or believes.

**Simplicity**  Keep it simple. Simplicity usually gets results. Keep both your presentations and thought processes simple.

**Situation**  Where you are in life is just where you happen to be at the moment. It is absolutely no indicator of what can or will be.

**Size**  It is not the size of the dog in the fight, it is the size of the fight in the dog.

**Skills**  Part of your job in life is to build, refine, update and focus your skills. There are no foolish questions. The only foolish thing is purposely not being informed.

**Sloppy**  Appearing sloppy or uncaring not only adds stress to those working with you but also shows a disrespect for them and their efforts.

**Slow Down**   Do not slow down or you might stop, and it is too difficult to get started again.

**Small**   If you think small, you will get small results.

**Smart**   Smart is not the same as wise. Smart people can do some really stupid things. Aim for wisdom. People who think they are smart think everyone else is stupid. That is their Achilles' heel.

**Smile**   Do it a lot, particularly at people who do not smile back. Everyone is more attractive when they are smiling. Smile as often as you can; it cheers others as well.

**Soccer**   One of the secrets to playing soccer well is not being afraid of getting kicked. This is also true in business and life generally.

**Sociopath**   This is someone who cannot understand how their actions affect others or events. A person devoid of conscience, empathy and responsibility. Sociopaths are, of course, full of excuses, rationalizations and self-justification. They are "users" and "takers" in their relationships. Do not deal with one.

Although most people are not clinical in this regard, many have this tendency. Examine yourself for this trait and try to eradicate it.

**Something** Generally, it is better to do something than nothing.

**Sorry** Do not be afraid to admit error and clean it up. It is a sign of character and trustworthiness.

A person has to be insecure or insular not to say "I'm sorry."

**Space** Give people, friends and family the space to be themselves, to grow, to achieve and even to fail.

**Special** Treat everyone as if they are special, because they are.

**Specific** People think in generalities but act specifically. For example, you may be attracted to a person but nothing happens until you ask for a date. In business, wanting to do business with someone must start with a specific offering or deal. Focus ideas into specifics.

**Speeches**  Keep speeches short, with just a couple of easy-to-remember takeaways.

**Speed**  This is not the same as productivity.

**Spending**  Spending money should not be one's focus in life.

**Spiritual**  The spiritual basis of a person's life is like the operating system of a computer. It is the how and why an individual conducts his or her life. It is also a point of reference or compass bearing in adversity.

Instead of bobbing like a cork from peak to trough, we are able to cut through adversity and grow. Spiritual vacuums do not exist. If you do not have a good operating basis, you have a flawed one.

**Spoiled**  Getting over being spoiled is hard. It must start with getting rid of a sense of entitlement, moving on to gratitude and finally thinking of others and their needs.

**Sportsmanship**  Sadly, sportsmanship has turned into winmanship.

**Stamina**  During hard times, work on keeping your spirit up. Try to quell fears and negative thinking.

Live in the present. Stay fit for the challenges that are going to come your way (physical, mental and spiritual).

**Standards**  The destruction of objective standards (e.g., right and wrong) eventually undercuts the moral behavior of individuals, corporations and nations.

"If you take the high road, you won't run into much traffic." – Warren Buffett

**Standing**  Any standing you have in your community, industry or company is not to be simply enjoyed or basked in. Standing should be used to do good things, to defend what is right. If that means putting some of that regard in which you are held at risk, do it. Standing is an asset to be used and invested. Not doing so will diminish your standing.

**Stand Up**  Not just for yourself, but for others. If you do not try to change what is wrong, you are part of the problem.

**Starting Over**  One starts over by stopping thinking they know everything.

**Starting Point**  The best starting point for success in business and life is to consider the needs and wants of others.

**Status**  "In the great quest for fame and fortune, aim for fortune and see if that doesn't cover most of what you want. There is no upside to fame."
– Bill Murray

**Stories**   We are all creating our own stories. How will yours read?

**Story**   Whenever there is a long or convoluted story about an opportunity or problem, don't buy any of it.

**Straight Line**   You cannot "straight line" the present into the future. There are always curves and surprises.

**Strength**   Strength comes from doing. You get better as you go. Strength and energy come from action, not the other way around. You haven't used all your strength until you have asked your God to help you.

**Stress**   Stress is unresolved conflict. Deal with it either in action or by changing your attitude toward the situation. Long-term stress is a killer.

**Strive**   Strive to become better – at everything.

**Structure**   Structure is required when respect, consideration and common sense are in short supply.

**Structures**  It is harder to create the structures for accumulating wealth than it is to make money. Structures provide the opportunity or means to capitalize on events.

**Stubborn**  Being stubborn can be good, if you are right. The problem is that most of us are not right all of the time. Ask yourself: "How important is it?" or "What is the real cost of being stubborn on an issue?"

Ask others for input as to the merits of your stance. Success often comes more from correcting mistakes quickly and limiting their damage than from being stubborn.

**Stupid**  If you see someone do something stupid while driving, stay away from them. They will probably do more stupid things.

**Subliminal**  Subliminal put-downs such as certain facial expressions or sighs while another is speaking are guaranteed to create enemies. They have career costs.

**Subsistence** Working simply to stay alive is not enough. We all need the hope that comes from building or accomplishing something.

**Substance** Substance is on the inside. It is what multiplies. The acorn is an example. One might see it simply as it is, or as a tree, or even as a forest. Aim at building substance in yourself and try to recognize it in others.

**Substitutes** Substitutes allow us to rationalize procrastination.

**Success** Success is the result of combining abilities with discipline. The bonding agent is the desire to succeed. This provides the motivation to grow in knowledge and skill – that is, to persevere in the things one must do for success. Too often, truly talented people fall by the wayside because of the inability or unwillingness to progress by working hard. Assume success, see yourself as successful and then act accordingly. Business success has two aspects: first, doing a thing well, and second, letting people know that you can do a thing well. (*See also* **Self-Image**.)

"Success" is a subjective matter. You decide on the goal that will give you the greatest fulfillment. Then work toward it.

**Successful**  To be successful in any business endeavor, you must be able to quell your emotions.

**Suffering**  "Suffering drives us out of the nursery of life in order to grow and feel love and life."
– C.S. Lewis

**Support**  Support your partners and associates. Not doing so is demoralizing and disrespectful.

**Surpass**  Go beyond what you have done before. Keep escalating your goals as you achieve them. Keep climbing.

**Survival**  Sometimes, survival depends upon the sheer imposition of your will. This is particularly true when the odds are heavily against you.

**Symptoms** Causes are more important than symptoms. Try to recognize the thinking and actions underlying outcomes.

Often what we see as problems are really symptoms.

# T

**Talk** If you talk down to people, you will not be an effective leader.

**Taxes** Do not make decisions on a purely tax basis. Invariably they will come back to haunt you. This includes wealth transfers to children.

**Teach** We teach people how to treat us. You have a part in the relationship.

**Teachable** Stay teachable. The learning process in business and life never ends. Income is directly related to being teachable.

**Team** Teams can accomplish much more than individuals. Function as a team member – passing the ball, giving credit and keeping other members informed. All teams require empathy, affinity and proximity.

Leaders build teams.

**Temptations**  Everyone has them. It is what one does or does not do about them that defines a person.

**Tenacity**  Sticking to a goal and a course of action, especially in adversity, is what success demands. You can refine as circumstances warrant, but stay on target.

**Tension**  Tension breeds more tension. Try to break that chain.

**Thank**  Thank people and God for all things, large and small. Everyone appreciates being appreciated.

**Theme**  If there is a recurring theme of disappointment or failure in your life, take a long serious look at your actions and attitudes.

**Things** Things have a tendency to replace relationships. Societies and individuals with little recognize the importance of friendship and connection. In the modern world, children spend far more time on their smartphone, tablet or computer than at even the odd, organized playdate. In the tug and pull between people and things, lean toward people.

**Thin Ice** Do not invest too much of yourself in relationships where you are continually on "thin ice," or expendable. Dependability and positive consistency are requisite for all worthwhile long-term relationships.

**Think** Think things through, not only directly to the intended goal but also to possible secondary and indirect outcomes, as well as to potential unintended consequences. One's line of reasoning and consideration should go further and wider than the initial desired objective.

**Thinking** If your thinking is off for an extended period of time, you start to think it is normal. As you think you will be.

**Thoughts** "No man can be a failure if he thinks he's a success." – Robert W. Service, *Making Good*

**Threats** Threats are always counterproductive. Leave the instruction, guidance or wish, without any threatening trailer.

Never threaten a person unless you are fully prepared to carry out the threat. If you are prepared to act, it is better not to give a warning.

**Time** Continuously move in the short term toward your longer-term goal. Stay on target, despite short-term distractions. Everything is "just for a time."

**Time Drains** Never underestimate the amount of your time others are prepared to waste. Time is a major asset. Don't fritter it away.

**Time Limits** Stick to the time requested for meetings. If you have asked for 15 minutes, then respect what you have been given, unless asked to stay longer.

If you stay within your self-imposed and stated limits, the door will usually be open in the future. If you do not, it probably will not be.

Meet deadlines for commitments or projects. Often you are part of a unit that must fit together on time. Advise of problems early.

**Time's Up**  It is a bit like a sell discipline in the stock market. It is knowing when things are over or about to be over. It is about change and a new direction. Don't be afraid of the signs. They lead to another adventure.

**Timing**  Timing is everything. Check the timing of your initiatives, actions and even statements.

**Tone**  How a leader treats one person sets the tone for a whole organization – for good or for ill.

**Toughness**  It is based upon what you can endure, not what you can inflict.

**Tough Times**  Tough times always present opportunities, even if it is simply the opportunity to be seen as positive and to show leadership.

If you do not learn from tough times, you are unteachable.

**Toys**  Toys do not add to our sense of self-worth. They are fun to have, but our accomplishments are more important.

**Transition**  Something new from something old. We often miss what is going on until after it has happened. Usually, all we sense at the time is difficulty or pain. Moving forward can be hard and frightening. As we look back, we can often see God's hand in our lives through changes in direction. The in-between times are sometimes hard, but they do not last.

**Travel**  We live in a global village. Travel, not as a tourist but to get understanding and build connections.

**Trends**  Try to spot them early in order to ride them or avoid their damage. This pertains to every business activity. Woolworths, Kresge and Sears all missed the Walmart trend to big box stores.

**Trigger Event**  Within every upset there is a trigger event that sets things off. Spotting it is the first step toward peace.

**Trouble**  To avoid trouble, stay seated.

**Trust**  J. P. Morgan once said, "If you can't trust a man, you shouldn't be dealing with him." Remember this when dealing with others, and work on being trustworthy yourself. Trust comes from consistency. Never trust a person who doesn't trust you. They are telling you about themselves.

**Truth**  Those who are not ready for the truth are usually ready to argue. Always deal in the truth. Don't bend it or skirt around it. Tell the truth in love, that is, with caring, not in anger. No one benefits from the latter.

# U

**Unconditional**  Loving and giving should always be unconditional, otherwise they are merely transactional. Love and give with no expectations.

**Underestimated**  Being underestimated can be a great advantage. The pressure to succeed comes only from you, and the opposition is off guard. Who would have thought in the '40s or '50s that Harry Truman would be remembered as one of the great American presidents?

German chancellor Helmut Kohl, the person most responsible for German reunification, claimed that being continually underestimated was one of his great advantages.

**Understand** How do others think? What motivates them? What are their fears and goals?

Strive to understand people, ideas and events.

**Understanding** Understanding is the wisdom to see potential outcomes. Leadership puts understanding to the test. If you do not understand something, chances are you are missing something – a piece of information or an intent.

**Unity** Leaders build unity. Self-serving individuals create division.

**Unkindness** Be neither actively nor coldly unkind. It is corrosive.

**Unmet Needs** These are the primary motivators for most people. If you can discern people's unmet needs, you will have insight into how they think and why they act the way they do. Work on this form of empathy in order to motivate people and to retain personal and business relationships.

**Unspeakable**  We all have an unspeakable secret, an irreversible regret, an intractable dream and an unforgettable love. These are parts of every life.

**Upset**  We always have a choice in this matter, to take offense or not. Look at the other person's heart or intent. Judge from experience rather than from one event. What is the real lesson? Then move on.

**Urgency**  Always have a sense of urgency when it comes to the tasks required for success.

**Use**  Use what is at hand better or smarter than those around you. Use what you have.

**Utilize**  Use and build on the skills you and your associates already have. Too often we launch into tangents, away from building on the strengths already in place.

# V

**Value** Offer value. Do not be stingy of spirit in your dealings. Try to add value to everything you are involved in.

**Values Conditioning** This is one of the most pernicious influences of media. Stand on your own integrity and be careful with compromising your values – especially the little compromises.

**Vengeance** The best vengeance is success. Use negative emotions as a spur for success.

**Victim** Many people go through life seeing themselves as victims. That sense of being a victim often leads to their becoming a victimizer. This holds for groups as well as for individuals.

**Vindictiveness** There is no room for vindictive behavior or thinking in a successful life.

**Virtual** You do not live in a virtual world. You live in a real one, with real people, real emotions and real outcomes.

**Virus** Just as a virus can infect the functioning of a computer, twisted thinking, bad attitudes and wrong values can impact our thinking. Take time out occasionally to check for and deal with viruses.

**Vision** Have a vision of what you seek to accomplish and a plan to achieve that vision. Then get on with it. All leaders have a vision of what can or should be.

**Vulnerability** A little vulnerability and a lot of forgiveness is a good formula for life.

# W

**Walk Out** Many people specialize in the "walk out." They continually walk out on relationships, careers, tasks and opportunities — on everything. An incident is usually the excuse, but the real motivation is often boredom, frustration, fear or any number of other reasons. This "geographical cure" can be life-long and it rarely works because we always keep taking ourselves with us. If you detect this pattern in your life, you are the problem.

**Wants** Occasionally, our "wants" are misplaced. Henry Ford once stated: "If I had given people what they wanted, I would have given them faster horses."

**Waste** If you are paying attention, very little is ever wasted. Time or money lost can often be profitable, if you learn the lesson of trying to get the best out of everything that happens in your life.

**Weak**  We are all weak from time to time. The support of loved ones and friends is immeasurable at those points. Be there for others, particularly when you also feel weak.

**Wealth**  You gain wealth by creating wealth or providing something valid for others.

**Wealthy**  If you want to know how wealthy you are, count the good things you have in your life that you cannot purchase with money.

**Willful**  It is near impossible to deal with self-will run riot. Distance yourself and dealings from individuals who act in this manner.

**Willpower**  Do not let your willpower undercut by others' "won't power."

**Winners**  Winners are not whiners.

**Winning** You are ready to start winning when you are ready to be both rigorous in your self-examination and willing to grow out of destructive thought patterns.

**With** All business success comes from working "with" people, not against them.

**Wolf Pack** The strength of the wolf is in the pack. The same is true of us.

**Word** If you give your word on anything, live up to it. Not doing so is an instant reputation destroyer. If your word doesn't matter, neither do you.

**Words** Words are important. They express thoughts, concepts and images. They have meaning. They convey ideas greater than their sum total, and occasionally different from one's intent. Don't throw them around carelessly. Strive for meaningful communication. Be clear.

**Work Smart** Work when you work and play when you play. Block out time to do both, but don't kid yourself by trying to do both at the same time.

Remember that failures use up more energy being failures than successes use being successes.

**Worry** Worry and the resulting stress are killers physically, emotionally, creatively and in many other ways. It is a habit and a form of addiction. There is always something to be positive or confident about.

**Worse** Assume others are having a worse day than you.

**Writing** Sometimes it is good to put our frustrations and hurts in a letter, as long as a wastebasket is nearby.

**Wrong** There is nothing wrong in being wrong, but there is with staying wrong.

**Wronged**  The nice part of being wronged is that it caters to our pride: "I would never do a thing like that." Before enjoying that moral superiority, one should consider their own part in the event.

# Y

**Yelling**   Never yell at anyone or anything. It gets you nowhere and accomplishes nothing. It is also destructive.

**Yet**   When you say you are not good at something, qualify it with the word "yet." With interest and effort, you can be good at anything.

**You**   You are responsible for you – no one else.

**Yourself**   Be yourself. Everyone else is already taken.

# Z

**Zeal** That enthusiastic sense of conviction or belief in what you are doing or trying to accomplish is a key ingredient for success. It must, however, be tempered with skill and understanding.

**Zzz** Get enough rest and sleep. Fatigue and fear go together. Vince Lombardi once said: "Fatigue makes cowards of us all." Be up for any task by being well rested. The same is true for getting enough exercise and proper nutrition.

# Notes

_____

_____

_____

_____

_____

_____

_____

_____